50 More Excel Functions

EXCEL ESSENTIALS BOOK 4

M.L. HUMPHREY

SELECT TITLES BY M.L. HUMPHREY

EXCEL ESSENTIALS
Excel for Beginners
Intermediate Excel
50 Useful Excel Functions
50 More Excel Functions

ACCESS ESSENTIALS
Access for Beginners
Intermediate Access

WORD ESSENTIALS
Word for Beginners
Intermediate Word

POWERPOINT ESSENTIALS
PowerPoint for Beginners
Intermediate PowerPoint

BUDGETING FOR BEGINNERS
Budgeting for Beginners
Excel for Budgeting

CONTENTS

INTRODUCTION

In *50 Useful Excel Functions* I explored the fifty Excel functions that I think are most useful for users who are new to Excel. But there are many, many functions in Excel that can be incredibly useful that I didn't even touch on in that book.

So in this guide we're going to cover another fifty Excel functions. The ones I've chosen for this guide include a number related to date or time calculations as well as some intermediate mathematical functions. You'll see, too, that with some of these functions you can get the same result without using a function. (When that's the case I'll mention what the alternative is.)

The next couple of chapters are for those readers who didn't read *50 Useful Excel Functions*. They cover the basics of how formulas and functions work in Excel. If you have already read *50 Useful Excel Functions* just skip right to the functions section because it's the same material you already read.

Keep in mind that which functions someone will find helpful will vary significantly based upon how they use Excel. In both books I've tried to keep to those functions where I think a larger proportion of people might use them, but there will be functions I discuss in here that you may never need and I am certain that there are probably functions I am not covering in either book that will be someone's go-to function. The beauty and the curse of Excel functions is in their variety.

Hopefully, however, you'll learn more about how to use functions in Excel after reading this book even if some of the functions are ones you don't ever need to use.

As with the rest of the books in this series, this book is written using Excel 2013. If you have a version of Excel prior to Excel 2007 your version of Excel will look and function very differently from the one I'm using. (At this point, it's probably worth upgrading.) There also may be functions that I cover that are not available to you. I will try to note that when I'm aware of it.

Also, if you're in a later version of Excel you may have access to functions that I don't. One thing I will caution you about with using the latest and greatest version of Excel is that not everyone will have it and so you may run into backwards compatibility issues. I spent many, many hours on a work project fixing a workbook to replace SUMIFS with a series of SUMIF functions when it turned out a client didn't have access to a version of Excel that was as current as the version of Excel I was working in. It was not fun.

So if you're the only one who will be using that workbook, use any function you want. But if you're going to be sharing that workbook and aren't sure what versions of Excel someone else has, be very careful to use functions that existed at least a few versions of Excel prior to the most recent one.

Okay then. The next few chapters will cover how formulas and functions work in Excel and then we'll dive straight in to the functions we're going to cover.

HOW FORMULAS AND FUNCTIONS WORK

If you are writing a basic mathematical formula in Excel you do so by starting your entry in a cell with a plus (+), a minus (-) or an equals (=) sign. Unless you have a good reason for doing so, like years of ingrained habit, I recommend just using the equals sign.

So if I want to add two values together in Excel, I would enter something like this into the cell:

=2+3

I could also do so using cell references if those values were already stored in cells in my worksheet:

=A1+B1

(If you aren't familiar with cell notation in Excel, see Appendix A.)

When I hit Enter or otherwise leave that cell, Excel will display the result of the formula in the cell. In the top example, that means it would display the value 5 in the cell. Excel will, however, retain the formula that was used to calculate that value. You can either double-click in the cell or click on the cell and look to the formula bar to see the formula.

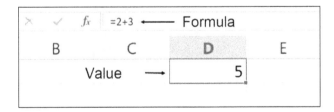

Excel formulas can use basic mathematical notation or they can use functions to perform specified tasks.

To add two numbers together in Excel you use the plus (+) sign between the values like I did above. To subtract one number from another you use the minus (-) sign. To multiply two numbers you use the asterisk (*) sign. To divide two numbers you use the forward slash (/). So:

=3-2 would subtract 2 from 3

=3*2 would multiply 3 times 2

=3/2 would divide 3 by 2

As I mentioned above, your formulas can either use cell references or numbers. So:

=A1-B1 would subtract the value in Cell B1 from the value in Cell A1

=A1*B1 would multiply the value in Cell A1 by the value in Cell B1

=A1/B1 would divide the value in Cell A1 by the value in Cell B1

Excel can handle as complex a formula as you want to throw at it. You can combine in one cell a formula that adds multiple values, divides values, subtracts values, and multiplies values as well as any number of other mathematical tasks or functions.

If you're going to combine calculation steps within one cell, you need to be careful that you properly place your parens so that calculations are performed in the correct order. There is a help document on this titled "Calculation operators and precedence in Excel" that lists the order in which calculations are done by Excel and also lists a number of operators (such as > for greater than) that are useful to know when working with formulas and functions in Excel.

If you're building a really complex formula it's always a good idea to test it as you go to make sure that all of the components are working properly and that the end result is the expected result. So I will build each component separately before combining them all in one cell.

Formulas in Excel go beyond the basic mathematical formula you learned in school. They can handle date-based, text-based, and logic-based calculations as well as mathematical calculations. They do this through the use of Excel functions.

Functions are essentially programmed shortcuts that do specific tasks. For example, the SUM function will add all of the values in a range of cells that you identify. Or the CONCATENATE function will take a set of inputs (usually text) and combine them together in one cell.

There are hundreds of functions in Excel that you can use in your formulas.

To use a function, you start a formula with the equals sign, type in the name of the function, use an opening paren, provide the inputs required for that function, and then use a closing paren.

So to sum a range of cells from A1 through A3 you would type

=SUM(A1:A3)

The equals sign tells Excel this is a formula, the SUM portion tells Excel that we're using the SUM function, the opening paren says we're going to list inputs for that function, the A1:A3 tell Excel which cells to apply the function to, and then the closing paren says that's the end of the function. It doesn't have to be the end of the formula.

(As we'll discuss at the end, you can combine functions within one formula.)

I could have

$$=SUM(A1:A3) + SUM(C1:C3)$$

That's sloppy notation. I could as easily have written =SUM(A1:A3,C1:C3) and had the same result. But the point here is that a formula starts with an equals sign and then you use functions as part of that formula by using their name followed by opening and closing parens and providing the required information for the particular function within the parens.

Don't worry. We're going to walk through lots and lots of examples of this. You'll get it if you don't now.

Just remember to think of a function, whether it handles text or is logical or performs a mathematical function, as part of a formula. In other words, as part of something that is being calculated based upon your inputs.

Garbage in, garbage out. If you give the function the wrong inputs, you will get the wrong results. So if you get an error message (which we'll discuss at the end) when using a function, check that the information you input into your formula is formatted properly and is of the right type. That's usually where things go wrong.

Alright. Next we'll talk about where to find functions in Excel. But remember, you need an equals sign (=) to start a formula and then you can use numbers, cell references, operators, or functions to build that formula.

WHERE TO FIND FUNCTIONS

In this guide we're going to cover fifty Excel functions, but there are far, far more functions than that in Excel. And chances are at some point you'll need one I didn't cover here.

In newer versions of Excel, you can go to the Formulas tab to see what Excel functions are available to you. There is a section called Function Library that lists various categories of functions. Mine shows Recently Used, Financial, Logical, Text, Date & Time, Lookup & Reference, Math & Trig, and then there's a dropdown for More Functions that shows the categories Statistical, Engineering, Cube, Information, Compatibility, and Web.

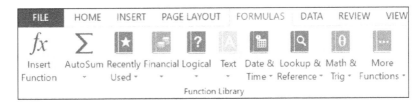

Click on the dropdown arrow next to any of the categories and you'll see a listing of functions that fall under that heading.

Now, unless you know what you're looking for, this listing probably won't help you much because the functions are named things like ACCRINT and IFNA. You can hold your cursor over each of the names and Excel will provide a brief description of the function for you, but for some of the lists that's a lot of functions to look through.

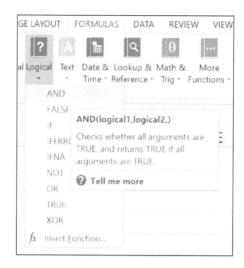

Each description also includes a Tell Me More at the end of the description. If you click on that option, the Excel Help screen will appear. You can then click on "Excel functions (alphabetical)" and choose your desired function from the list. This will show you additional information on the function and how it works.

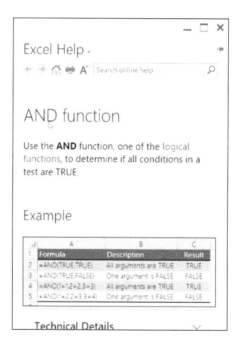

Instead of that, I would recommend that you use the Insert Function option which is also available in the Formulas tab on the far left-hand side.

Be sure you're clicked into an empty cell on your worksheet and then click on Insert Function. This will bring up the Insert Function dialogue box.

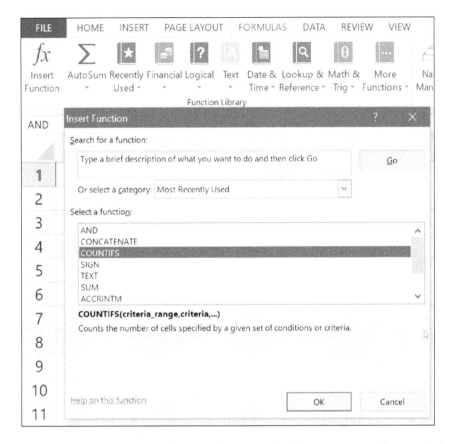

In the top section under where it says "Search for a function" you can type what you're looking to do and then click on Go. (Be sure that the category dropdown right below the search box is set to All unless you know for certain what category your function falls under.)

Excel will provide a list of functions that it thinks meet your search criteria. (Sometimes this list is very far off, so don't just accept the first choice blindly.) You can left-click on each of the listed functions to see a brief description of the function. This appears below the box where the functions are listed.

You will also see for each function a list of the required inputs for that function.

For COUNTIFS you can see in the screenshot above that the first input required is the criteria range and that the second input required is the criteria and that the description of the function is "Counts the number of cells specified by a given set of conditions or criteria."

(In this guide I have listed this information for each function at the top of the function's page.)

If you need more information on a function, you can click on the "Help on this function" link in the bottom left corner of the dialogue box. This will bring up the Excel Help box for that particular function.

Otherwise, you can just click on the function you want and choose OK.

This will insert the function into whichever cell you'd been clicked into before you chose Insert Function. You will also see a Function Arguments dialogue box that lists the inputs your function needs and provides a location for you to input those values.

You can either input numeric values in those boxes or use cell references by clicking on the cells in your worksheet or typing the cell references in.

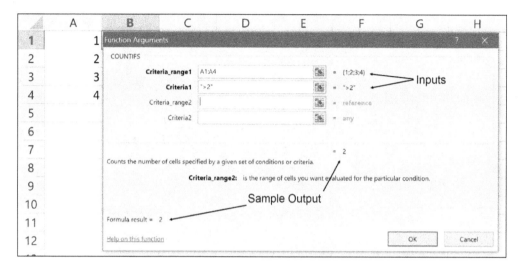

At the bottom of the list of inputs Excel will show you a sample value based upon the inputs you've chosen. The sample also appears in the bottom left corner of the dialogue box.

When you're done, click OK.

* * *

If you already know the function you want to use but aren't sure about the inputs, you can start typing your formula into a cell. After you type equals and the function name you will see a definition for the function.

After you type the opening paren for the function you will see a description of the inputs needed for the function listed.

1	=countif(
2	COUNTIF(**range**, criteria)
3	

If you click on the function name in that description after you've typed the opening paren, Excel will open the Excel Help dialogue box specific to that function.

* * *

If none of that works to help you find the function you need, then an Internet search is probably your best option.

A quick search for something like "How do I get Excel to identify the day of the week from a date?" will usually get you the answer you need. You can then use the Excel help for that formula either from within Excel or from the Microsoft website to guide you. (Or watch a free video on how to do it.)

* * *

One final note.

In older versions of Excel the Formulas tab didn't exist, so what I would do to bring up that Insert Function dialogue box is I would type equals into a cell and then go to the white dropdown box to the left of the formula bar, click on that dropdown arrow, and choose More Function from the bottom of the list.

This would bring up the Insert Function dialogue box and then I could follow the steps above.

So that's how you find the functions you need, what they do, and what inputs they require.

FORMULA AND FUNCTION BEST PRACTICES

Now let's discuss a few best practices when it comes to using formulas and functions.

Make Your Assumptions Visible

You're going to see as we move forward that you can build a formula that uses a function where all of the information to make the calculation is contained within that one cell.

So if I want to add the values 10, 20, and 30 together I can do that in one cell using the SUM function, =SUM(10,20,30), and all anyone will see in the worksheet is the result of that calculation, 60.

You may be tempted to do this because it's clean. All that people see is what you want them to, the result of your calculation.

And maybe you don't expect to have to adjust those values so you don't see an issue in having your formula built that way.

I would encourage you not to do this. In my experience, a best practice in terms of building formulas is to have any fixed values or assumptions visible in the worksheet. The reason to do this is so that someone looking at the sheet can see what assumptions fed the calculation.

Here's an example:

Let's say you're calculating how much you'll make if you sell your house. You figure you'll have to spend $2,500 to clean the place up a bit, pay a commission of 5%, and that the house is worth $500,000.

Now, if you sat down to discuss this with your spouse you could just show them the results of that calculation (the value on the left) or you could show them the results of the calculation and the assumptions you made (the value on the right).

	A	B	C	D	E
1		Option 1			Option 2
2				Home Price	$500,000.00
3	Net	$ 472,500.00		Commission	5%
4				Fix Up Cost	$2,500.00
5					
6				Net	$472,500.00
7					

Option 2 is more useful, because you can both see what assumptions were made and acknowledge and validate each one. Maybe your spouse knows that houses in the area have been selling for $400,000 instead of $500,000 or that the neighbors up the street worked with a great broker who only charges 4% commission. Without showing them your assumptions, they aren't given a chance to provide their input.

If you bury your assumptions in your calculation field they're easy to forget about. And that can be dangerous if they're wrong.

So I strongly urge you to always have your assumptions present and visible in your worksheet rather than buried in your formulas.

Use Paste Special - Values

The other thing I do that you may or may not want to do depending on why you're using Excel is that I frequently use Paste Special – Values when I'm done with performing a set of calculations.

Do not do this if the calculations you performed need to be updated on an ongoing basis.

But I do a lot of calculations where I want to keep the results for reference but will not be recalculating any values. In this case I want to lock those values down so that I don't lose them or inadvertently recalculate them by changing a value in an input cell or deleting data that fed those calculations.

The simple way to do this is to select the cells, Ctrl + C to copy, and then right-click and under Paste Special choose the Values option (the one with the 123 on the clipboard). This will replace any calculated cells in that range with just the values of the calculation.

After you do that, instead of a formula that says "add Cells A1 and B1 together" you'll have a cell that just contains the result of having added Cells A1 and B1 together. Now if you delete Cells A1 and B1 or change their values, your result field won't change.

Don't Mess With Your Raw Data

I mentioned this in the other books, but am going to mention it again here.

To the extent possible, you should always store your raw data in one location and do all of your calculations and manipulations on that data elsewhere. (Ideally you would also record all of the steps you followed to take that raw data and turn it into your final product, but it's not as easy to do in something like Excel as it is in a program like R.)

If you don't do this, all it takes is one bad sort or one bad function and your data can be irreparably changed if you don't catch it right away.

If you keep your raw data separate there is nothing you can't come back from. You might have to redo a lot of work, but you won't be left with a dataset that's useless.

I also save versions of my worksheets when I'm working on something particularly complicated. That way I can go back to a stage where everything was working without having to start over from scratch. Just be sure to label your files clearly so that you know which is the most recent version. (File V1, File V2, etc.)

Test Your Formulas

If I'm going to apply a formula to a large range of data I will usually test that formula on a much smaller sample of my data where I can visually evaluate the results. So if I'm writing a formula to sum customer transactions for customers from Alaska who bought Widgets (using SUMIFS), I'll run that formula against just ten rows of data to make sure that it's doing what I think it should before I apply it to ten thousand rows of data.

As much as possible you should always either check you formulas on a subset of data or "gut check" your results. Don't just accept the value Excel gives you without questioning whether it actually makes sense. (Because garbage in, garbage out. Excel's ability to perform calculations is limited by your ability to write those calculations properly. And we all make mistakes. One missing $ sign or one > instead of >= and the result you get will not be the result you wanted.)

Test, test, test. And then check, check, check.

COPYING FORMULAS

Before we move into discussing specific functions, I want to cover how to copy formulas and keep cell references fixed.

One of the most powerful aspects of Excel, for me, is in the fact that I can write a formula once, copy it, and paste it to thousands of cells, and it will automatically adjust to its new location

It's fantastic.

When that's what you want.

When copying a formula always check the formula first to be sure that it's going to copy well.

The biggest issue I run into with copying formulas is failing to lock down cells that need to be fixed references.

So if I've put interest rate in Cell A1 and I need every single calculation no matter the row to reference Cell A1, then I need to lock down that cell reference before I copy the formula. You do this by using $ signs in your formula.

To lock an entire cell reference use dollar signs in front of both the column and the row identifier. So $A$1 will always reference the cell in Column A and Row 1 no matter where I copy that formula to.

To lock just the column reference, put a dollar sign in front of the column identifier. So $A1. This will ensure that no matter where the formulas is copied to, that cell will always reference Column A. The row number, however, will be able to adjust. (I use this in my two-variable analysis grid.)

To lock the row reference, put a dollar sign in front of the row identifier. So A$1. This will ensure that no matter where the formula is copied to, the cell will always reference Row 1. The column reference, however, will change.

I find that when I'm copying formulas I need to check for not only fixed values, like the interest rate example above, but also for cell ranges.

For example, if I want to know what percent of my overall sales each product was and I have a list of sales by product I can calculate that by taking the sales for each product divided by the total sales for all products. If I take that total sales by referencing a cell range, such as A1:A25, then before I copy that formula down my row of values I need to lock in that range by writing it as $A$1:$A$25.

If I don't do that, in the next row down that cell range will change to be A2:A26 instead of A1:A25.

So always check before copying.

And if you just need to move a formula to a new location but don't want any of the cell references to adjust then you need to cut and move the formula instead of copying it.

OK. That's it for the preliminaries. Time to start talking about specific functions. We'll start with some basic Math & Trig ones first.

THE IFNA FUNCTION

Notation: IFNA(value,value_if_na)
Excel Definition: Returns the value you specify if the expression resolves to #N/A, otherwise returns the result of the expression.

The IFNA function is one that I didn't include in *50 Useful Excel Functions* even though I could have. The reason I didn't include it in the first fifty functions I covered is because I'm so comfortable with using IF functions that I just quickly write an IF function that does what IFNA does without looking to see if a function exists to do what I want, which is suppress that pesky #NA! result that sometimes occurs.

But I found myself using this the other day and it's very straight-forward and easy to use. The way it works is that you tell it a function to perform and if the result of that function is the #N/A! error then instead of returning that error you can specify what Excel returns instead.

(I say function here, but the Excel help text calls it an argument.)

The easiest way to show how this works is to walk you through an example.

Let's say I have a list of my books I've published and how much I've spent on ads for those books each month. I also have a list of how much I've earned for each book each month. And I decide I want to combine those two sets of information to calculate a profit/loss per month for each book.

I can use the CONCATENATE function to create an entry for both data sets that combines month-year-title into one column and then use VLOOKUP to look up the amount I spent on ads for each title in each month and bring that into the sales worksheet.

But when VLOOKUP can't find an entry—so in months where I had book sales but no ad spend, for example—Excel returns a value of #N/A! When that happens within a column of data you can no longer click on that column and see its summed value. This would prevent me from checking that I'd captured all of my ad costs.

But I can easily fix this issue using the IFNA function.

If my original formula was:

=VLOOKUP(D:D,'Advertising Spend By Series'!E:F,2,FALSE)

(That's saying look for the value in Column D of this worksheet in Column E of the Advertising Spend by Series tab and then pull the value from Column F, but only if the two values are an exact match.)

The revised formula using IFNA is:

=IFNA(VLOOKUP(D:D,'Advertising Spend By Series'!E:F,2,FALSE),0)

That looks complicated, but it's not. Replace the VLOOKUP portion with an X and you have:

=IFNA(X,0)

Basically, if there's a value for VLOOKUP to return then return that value, otherwise return a zero.

I chose to return a value of zero, but you could easily have it return a text statement instead. If you are going to have it return text, be sure to use quotation marks around the text you want returned. So if I wanted "No Match" returned instead of a zero, I'd use:

=IFNA(VLOOKUP(D:D,'Advertising Spend By Series'!E:F,2,FALSE),"No Match")

If you don't want anything returned, so you just want an apparently blank cell, then leave that second argument blank. You'll still need to use the comma, so it should look like this:

=IFNA(VLOOKUP(D:D,'Advertising Spend By Series'!E:F,2,FALSE),)

That will return a value of "" in that cell instead of the #N/A! error message.

That's it.

It looks a little complicated because we were working with a VLOOKUP function, but it's really very simple.

Take the formula you already have that's giving you the #N/A! results, type IFNA(between the equals sign and that first function, go to the end, add a comma, put in the result you want returned when there's an N/A result (if any), and then add a closing paren. Done.

Just keep in mind, of course, that you will not see an #N/A! result if you use this function, which could hide from you valuable information about your calculation or your data.

Also, it's particular to just that type of error. Other error messages, such as #DIV/0!, will still be displayed.

If you want to suppress all error messages, then you need to use IFERROR which we'll discuss next.

THE IFERROR FUNCTION

Notation: IFERROR(value,value_if_error)
Excel Definition: Returns value_if_error if expression is an error and the
value of the expression itself otherwise.

The IFERROR function is just like the IFNA function except that it will return your specified value for any error message, not just the #N/A! error message. Error messages suppressed by the function include: #N/A!, #VALUE!, #REF!, #DIV/0!, #NUM!, #NAME?, and #NULL!

So be sure before you use it that you are okay with suppressing all of those error messages. For example, the #REF! error message usually will tell you when you've deleted a cell that was being referenced by a formula. That for me isn't something I would like to hide. If I've made that mistake, I want to know it.

But if you have a range of cells with a formula in them that's returning, for example, the #DIV/0! error because you're currently dividing by zero, which is an issue I've run into in some of my worksheets, this might be a good option.

Your other option is to use a simple IF function instead.

For example, I use

$$=IF(P1=0,"",J1/P1)$$

in one of my worksheets, because it returns a #DIV/0! error until P1 has a value and that annoys me. IFERROR would work the same in that situation. I could use

$$=IFERROR(J1/P1,)$$

instead. Note that I left the second argument, the value_if_error empty which will return a blank cell as long as dividing the value in Cell J1 by the value in Cell P1 produces an error message. To do that I still had to include the comma, though.

My temptation in using either IFNA or IFERROR is to have them return zeroes or empty cells, but I would recommend that if you're using IFERROR in a crucial situation that you have it return a text entry instead so that you always know when there's an error message that's being suppressed.

So

$$=IFERROR(J1/P1,"No\ Value")$$

is probably a better choice than

$$=IFERROR(J1/P1,)$$

because you will know for a fact that the formula generated an error message and won't think that the value in that cell was entered as zero.

Note above that I used quotes around the text I wanted to have Excel display in the place of my error message, just like I did with IFNA.

THE NOT FUNCTION

Notation: NOT(logical)
Excel Definition: Changes FALSE to TRUE, or TRUE to FALSE.

This next one, the NOT function, is one I'm including only because Microsoft themselves highlight it as useful. Also, it is related to the AND and OR functions, which I do think you should know, that I already covered in *50 Useful Excel Functions*.

But the fact of the matter is that my psychology background tells me that using a negative to build a function is a bad idea and I would encourage you to find another way to accomplish your goal if you're ever tempted to use the NOT function.

At its most basic, the NOT function returns the opposite result. So

$$=NOT(FALSE)$$

returns a value of TRUE. And

$$=NOT(TRUE)$$

returns a value of FALSE.

But you're never going to use it that way.

Where you might want to use it is to evaluate whether a criteria was met.

So let's say that I have two criteria that must be met for someone to be given a bonus. They have to have been employed for over 12 months and they have to have generated over $25,000 in sales.

I could use a NOT function to ask if that happened. So, was my employee's time with the company in Cell B5 greater than 12 months? To do this, I'd write

$$=NOT(B5<12)$$

to get a result of FALSE when the employee had not been there at least 12 months and a result of TRUE if they had.

See how I had to do less than 12 there to get the right result?
I could have just as easily used an IF function instead and written

$$=IF(B5>12,TRUE)$$

to get the same result without the mental gymnastics using the NOT function requires.

In the Excel help text for this function, they give a different bonus scenario and then write a really ugly looking formula to calculate the bonus. It looks like this:

$$=IF(AND(NOT(B14<\$B\$7),NOT(C14<\$B\$5)),B14*\$B\$8,0)$$

But let me flip that around for you by removing the NOT function and switching the less than signs to greater than signs. If I do that I get:

$$=IF(AND(B14>=\$B\$7,C14>=\$B\$5),B14*\$B\$8,0)$$

It returns the same result as using the NOT function but with a lot less headache. (Just be sure to test that border case of equals to B7 and B5 to make sure you get it exactly right...I had initially written it as > instead of >=, a common problem I have to watch out for.)

Bottom line with the NOT function: If you're ever tempted to use it ask yourself if there isn't a different and simpler way to do what you're trying to do. I'm not going to say that there's absolutely no possible use for this function, but I am pretty confident in saying that ninety-nine times out of a hundred you should be able to find an alternate way of doing your calculation that doesn't require you to use the NOT function.

But for that remaining one in a hundred scenario, now you know how to use it.

THE HLOOKUP FUNCTION

Notation: HLOOKUP(lookup_value, table_array, row_index_num, [range_lookup])
Excel Definition: Looks up a value in the top row of a table or array of values and returns the value in the same column from a row you specify.

While we're covering functions that relate to ones already covered in *50 Useful Excel Functions*, let's go over HLOOKUP. You'll notice that it has a very similar name to VLOOKUP, which is a function my friends swear by. (I'm coming around on it. It was recently very handy, but mostly because my data happened to be arranged in a way that I could use it without massive changes.)

Where VLOOKUP scans down a column to match your value and then pulls a result from another column in the row where the match was made, HLOOKUP scans across a row to match your value and then pulls a result from another row in that column where the match was made.

So it's a transposed version of VLOOKUP.

VLOOKUP is the much more popular of the two options because of how most people structure their data. But let's say I have a table of data with month across the top and vendor across the left-hand side and I want to extract how much was earned on a specific vendor in a specific month. I could do that using HLOOKUP.

Here's our example data table:

	A	B	C	D	E	F	G	H	I	J	K	L	M
1		January	February	March	April	May	June	July	August	September	October	November	December
2	Amazon	$100.00	$107.00	$114.49	$122.50	$131.08	$140.26	$150.07	$160.58	$171.82	$183.85	$196.72	$210.49
3	Createspace	$37.00	$39.59	$42.36	$45.33	$48.50	$51.89	$55.53	$59.41	$63.57	$68.02	$72.78	$77.88
4	ACX	$23.50	$25.15	$26.91	$28.79	$30.80	$32.96	$35.27	$37.74	$40.38	$43.20	$46.23	$49.46
5	Con Sales	$10.00			$25.00		$8.00		$100.00			$23.00	
6	Apple	$48.50	$37.00	$52.30	$131.08	$39.59	$42.36	$45.33	$43.97	$42.65	$41.37	$40.13	$38.92
7	Authors Republic	$51.89	$40.48	$31.57	$140.26	$116.41	$96.62	$80.20	$66.56	$55.25	$45.86	$38.06	$31.59
8	D2D	$55.53	$43.31	$33.78	$150.07	$124.56	$103.39	$85.81	$71.22	$59.11	$49.06	$40.72	$33.80
9	Google	$59.41	$46.34	$36.15	$160.58	$133.28	$110.62	$91.82	$76.21	$63.25	$52.50	$43.57	$36.17
10	Kobo	$25.15	$26.91	$28.79	$30.80	$25.57	$21.22	$17.61	$14.62	$12.13	$10.07	$8.36	$6.94
11	Nook	$37.74	$40.38	$43.20	$46.23	$38.37	$31.85	$26.43	$21.94	$18.21	$15.11	$12.54	$10.41
12	Pronoun	$25.15	$26.91	$28.79	$18.71	$12.16	$7.91	$5.14	$3.34	$2.17	$1.41	$0.92	$0.60

If I use the formula:

=HLOOKUP("April",B1:M12,4,FALSE)

25

that will look for a value for the month of April in the table contained in Cells B1 through M12 and will return the value from the fourth row of that table (ACX) for that month. A value will only be returned if there is an exact match to "April" in the first row of the table range I specified.

Let's break this down further.

The first entry in any HLOOKUP formula is going to be what you're looking up. This can be a numeric value, a text string, or a cell reference. In the example above, because I wanted to look up a specific text value, I had to use quotation marks.

With text entries, if you're looking for an exact match you can also use the wildcards that Excel has for text lookups. A question mark means any one character and an asterisk means any number of characters. So "*April" would search for any text string that has April at the end whereas "?April" would only search for any text string that has one character before ending in April.

(You can use a tilde sign (~) before a question mark or asterisk if you actually want to search for an asterisk or question mark and not use it as a wildcard.)

The second input into the HLOOKUP function is where you're going to search. That's the table array. The first row of that table array is where what you're searching for needs to be. The table array then has to have the row with the values you want to return somewhere below the search row. (This is where VLOOKUP always fails me. My data is rarely structured the way it needs to be to use VLOOKUP. But I suspect with HLOOKUP this would be less of a problem.)

With HLOOKUP (as with VLOOKUP), there are two options for what you're searching for. You can search for an exact match or you can search for an approximate match. If you choose to search for an approximate match, then your data in the lookup row needs to be sorted in ascending order for HLOOKUP to work properly. If you're looking for an exact match then the order of the entries doesn't matter.

When looking up values Excel treats uppercase and lower case entries as the same. It is not case sensitive.

(As a side note, you can sort the columns of a table using the Sort function in Excel. It's not something I covered in *Excel for Beginners* or *Intermediate Excel* because it's not something most people do, but it's there in the Sort dialogue box. You can change the Options choice to Sort Left to Right.)

The third value that you need to provide for any HLOOKUP function is which row to pull your results from. This is which row within the range of data you provided as the table array. So it is not the actual row number. It's which row within your specified data table that you want to pull from.

If you provide a negative number, you'll get an error message. If you provide a value that is larger than the size of the range you specified, you will also get an error message.

If you provide a value of 1 that will return either the value you were looking up (for an exact match) or the closest possible value (for an approximate match), which can be especially useful if you want the closest value to what you're looking up. (Although I suspect this is more likely to be useful with VLOOKUP than HLOOKUP.)

The final input into the function is optional. This is where you tell Excel whether you want an exact match or an approximate match. If you omit this input, Excel will look for an approximate match so will return a result for the value that's closest to what you were looking for. It defines closest by which value is the next largest without going over the value you were looking for.

If you use FALSE for this input, then Excel will look for an exact match only and return #N/A! if there is no match.

You will also get an #N/A! error if you ask for an approximate match but the lookup value you specify is smaller than the smallest value in the table.

If you do get an error message, check your spelling, that your table range is correct, and that your row references are correct. If that all looks good, then you can look at the help function for HLOOKUP to see which error message you received and what that might mean.

Where VLOOKUP to me seems to be best used for looking up values in a table, like a discount table, I see HLOOKUP as most useful when you want to extract data from an existing summary table like in the example I gave above. But the two do operate on the same principles, so if you understand how to use one you should be able to use the other as well.

THE TRANSPOSE FUNCTION

Notation: TRANSPOSE(array)
Excel Definition: Converts a vertical range of cells to a horizontal range, or vice versa.

The TRANSPOSE function is one that you probably won't use very often, but I wanted to cover it because it actually came up in *50 Useful Excel Functions*.

So let's walk through what TRANSPOSE does. It takes a series of entries that are in a column and displays them in a row instead or takes a series of entries that are in a row and displays them in a column. You can do this with a combination of rows and columns as well. It will basically flip those entries so that what was in columns is now in rows and what was in rows is now in columns.

TRANSPOSE is a special kind of function that Excel introduced called an array formula. There are two key things to remember when working with array formulas. First, you need to select a range of cells before you start typing your formula in or it won't work. Second, you need to use Ctrl + Shift + Enter when you're done entering your formula or it also won't work. These two steps are what, for me, distinguish array formulas from other formulas. (That and the fact that the values they return appear in a range of cells instead of a single cell, of course.)

Let's walk through an example:

In Cells A1 through A6 type the numbers 1 through 6.

Now, go to Cell E6 and highlight Cells E6 through J6. (These are the cells we want to paste that data into.)

Keeping those cells highlighted, start typing your formula which is

=TRANSPOSE(A1:A6)

Finish with Ctrl + Shift + Enter.

If you've done it right, you should now see the numbers 1 through 6 in Cells E6 through J6. If you click on one of those cells, the formula in the formula bar should look like this:

{=TRANSPOSE(A1:A6)}

Those squiggly brackets indicate an array formula.

Keep in mind, too, that for this to work the range of cells you select for your function have to be the same size as what you're transposing but in the opposite direction. So if you have a table that is four columns across and three rows down that you want to transpose, you need to select a range of cells that is four rows down and three columns across.

Now, the other option if you just want to change the orientation of your data is to copy and then use Paste Special-Transpose. To do this, select the cells you want to copy, click in the first cell where you want to paste that data (making sure enough cells are empty so you're not over-writing anything), and then right click, and under Paste Options choose the Transpose option. (The one with two little two-box grids with an arrow pointing between them in the bottom right corner of the clipboard image. For me, right now, that's the fourth image choice.)

(In older versions of Excel you can do this using the Paste Special dialogue box and clicking in the Transpose box at the bottom on the right-hand side.)

So if you can just copy and Paste Special-Values, why would you want to use this TRANSPOSE function instead? The key difference is that when you TRANSPOSE your data using the function it is still linked to the original source. So if you change the values in those original cells, the transposed data will update as well. If you use Paste Special – Transpose, that data is not linked anymore. You are just pasting in the values and if you update your original data it will do nothing to what you pasted.

Also, the use we saw in *50 Useful Excel Functions* was built into a formula that would have normally returned results in a column. By using TRANSPOSE as part of that formula we were able to have the results returned across a row. So if you're working with other array formulas, TRANSPOSE allows you to change whether results appear across a row or down a column.

Basically, which option (function or pasting) is the better choice will depend on why you needed to do that. If you just wanted to transform a row of data into a column or vice versa, which is my usual reason for doing this, then Paste Special – Transpose is the easiest choice. If you're wanting to change the orientation of data that's output from an array formula or you want to copy data from one source and paste it to another in a different orientation while keeping the two sources linked, then the TRANSPOSE function will be the better option.

Just remember that when you use it it's an array formula so has to be set up and completed in a different manner than a normal formula does, namely by highlighting your range of cells in advance and by finishing with Ctrl + Shift +Enter.

THE INDEX FUNCTION

Notation: INDEX(array,row_num,[column_num])
or
INDEX(reference,row_num,[column_num],[area_num])

Excel Definition: Returns a value or reference of the cell at the intersection of a particular row and column, in a given range.

The INDEX function can take two forms. It can be an array formula and return a range of values like we just saw TRANSPOSE do, or it can serve as a basic lookup formula and return a value in a specified column and row within a specified table.

I will note here that at least in Excel 2013 when you open the help box for this function that it links to a video which gives a very nice overview of both ways of using the INDEX function, so I'd encourage you to watch that. But I'm going to walk through it here, too, so you don't have to if you don't want to.

At its most basic, the reference version

=INDEX(reference,row_num,[column_num],[area_num])

looks for a specific value in a specified position in a table. (To me this is much like how VLOOKUP and HLOOKUP work except it's not looking for a match to a value but just a specific position.)

The first argument you provide in this version is the table you want to look in. Let's say you have student grades for a series of tests and the data table is in Cells A2 through E7 with the actual data in Cells B3 through E7. Like so:

	A	B	C	D	E
1		Semester 1			
2		Test 1	Test 2	Test 3	Test 4
3	Student A	82	87	94	92
4	Student B	88	81	84	83
5	Student C	65	68	64	63
6	Student D	98	98	98	99
7	Student E	86	88	84	83

If you want to extract from that table the grade on the third test for Student B, you could write either of the two following formulas using the INDEX function:

=INDEX(A2:E7,3,4)

or

=INDEX(B3:E7,2,3)

The difference between these two is the range of cells I told Excel to use for the reference data table. In the first one, I included the header row and column with the student names, Cells A2 through E7. In the second I just included the results, Cells B3 through E7. That's the first input into the INDEX function. The data range to use.

The second input is which row *in that range* to pull the data from. (This is where it's like VLOOKUP and HLOOKUP, because those work the same way.) This is not the actual row number in the worksheet. This is which row in your chosen range to pull from. So when I include the header row, Student B's data is in the third row of the data range. When I don't include the header row Student B's data is in the second row of the data range.

The third input is which column *in that range* to pull the data from. Same concept. Because in the first example I included the student names column, then to pull data for the third test we need to look at the fourth column in the data range. But in the second example where I only included the results, we pull from the third column.

There is a fourth input option that the INDEX function can use. It is very well demonstrated in that video that I referenced above, but I'll walk through it here as well.

The fourth input option works when you have more than one data table to look up values in. To use this option, the first input for the function has to include more than one data range. If you include more than one range in that first input then you can use the fourth input option for INDEX to tell Excel which of the multiple ranges you provided it should use.

(If you have not provided multiple ranges and specify a number for this fourth input you will get a #REF! error.)

The example they use is four tables where you have different sales values for different regions and different time periods for different products and want to pull the information for sales in the same region and time period for each of four products.

I'm going to use a different scenario here. Let's say that you teach the same group of students for two different semesters and so have test results for both of those semesters for the same students. Like this:

	A	B	C	D	E
1		Semester 1			
2		Test 1	Test 2	Test 3	Test 4
3	**Student A**	82	87	94	92
4	**Student B**	88	81	84	83
5	**Student C**	65	68	64	63
6	**Student D**	98	98	98	99
7	**Student E**	86	88	84	83
8					
9		Semester 2			
10		Test 1	Test 2	Test 3	Test 4
11	**Student A**	88	92	93	96
12	**Student B**	90	83	85	85
13	**Student C**	62	62	62	62
14	**Student D**	65	65	68	66
15	**Student E**	91	92	93	95

And now you want to pull the test score for the same student for the third test for each semester.

First, let's pull the same data we pulled above, but with the INDEX formula set up to pull from either table, and specifying which table to use.

We can rewrite both formulas to include both table ranges and to pull from the first table like so:

=INDEX((A2:E7,A10:E15),3,4,1)

or

=INDEX((B3:E7,A10:E15),2,3,1)

Now we can modify both of those formulas to pull a value from the second table instead by changing the value of the last input in the function:

$$=INDEX((A2:E7,A10:E15),3,4,2)$$

or

$$=INDEX((B3:E7,A10:E15),2,3,2)$$

Of course, the way I would actually use this is not by manually going in and changing that final number each time. I would instead build a table that pulls in values from each semester. Like this:

	I	J	K	L
8		**Test 3 Results**		
9				
10			**Semester**	
11			**1**	**2**
12	**Student A**	1	94	93
13	**Student B**	2	84	85

The formula I used here in Cell K12 is:

$$=INDEX((\$A\$2:\$E\$7,\$A\$10:\$E\$15),(\$J12+1),4,K\$11)$$

That says that there are two tables of data to pull from, that the row to use is equal to the number in Column J plus 1, that the column to use is the fourth one, and that the table to pull from is the table number in Row 11. I can then just copy that formula down to the other four cells and it will populate my table for me by looking in each of the semester grade tables for each student.

That to me has some potential value in extracting information from multiple tables to create a summary table.

The other potential value of the INDEX function is in its ability to pull an entire row or column of data out of a table. That is done by treating it as an array formula.

Remember from looking at the TRANSPOSE function that there are a few key things you need to do to treat a function as an array formula. You have to select a range of cells not just one cell and then you have to use Ctrl + Shift + Enter after you've created the formula.

So let's go back to our two tables of data and let's extract all of the test scores for Student A using INDEX as an array formula, one row per semester

In Columns I, J, and K and Rows 17 and 18 I've created a simple table with my semester number and my student row number so that I can use cell references to do this.

Once I've done that I can highlight Cells L17 through O17 and then in L17 put the formula:

$$=INDEX((\$B\$3:\$E\$7,\$B\$11:\$E\$15),J17,0,K17)$$

I finish by using Ctrl + Shift + Enter.

I can then repeat that with Cells L18 through O18 to pull grades for the same student for the second semester. What I end up with is something that looks like this:

	I	J	K	L	M	N	O
16			Semester				
17	**Student A**	1	1	82	87	94	92
18		1	2	88	92	93	96

Let's look at the formula again:

$$=INDEX((\$B\$3:\$E\$7,\$B\$11:\$E\$15),J17,0,K17)$$

What this is saying is that there are two tables to choose from, one in Cells B3 through E7 and one in Cells B11 through E15 and that I want to pull the data from the row specified in Cell J17. (Since we're just looking at the data and no header row, it can continue to reference the first row and not need to adjust.)

It then says that there is no column to pull from and that I want to do this from the data table specified in Cell K17.

I can then use that formula in Cell L18, adjusting for the row number with J17 and K17 becoming J18 and K18, to pull in the scores from the second data table for that student.

(I will note here that you can't just copy and paste that second formula down like you would with a normal formula. It took a little fiddling to get it to copy down properly for me.)

In the same way that we extracted a row from a data table, you can also extract a column. Just make the row value 0 and provide a column value instead. Also, make sure that you highlight the number of cells needed in a specific column instead of in a row.

And, to circle back to our TRANSPOSE function, if you wanted to return the column values as a row, you could pair the INDEX function with the TRANSPOSE function. So you could highlight five cells within a row and then use:

$$=TRANSPOSE(INDEX((\$B\$3:\$E\$7,\$B\$11:\$E\$15),0,3,1))$$

to pull the third column of data from the table of data contained in Cells B3 through E7.

Keep in mind that these are still formulas, so if you change your source data you will change the values that you've pulled from the table. To lock any values into place use Paste Special – Values.

THE MATCH FUNCTION

Notation: MATCH(lookup_value,lookup_array,[match_type])
Excel Definition: Returns the relative position of an item in an array that matches
a specified value in a specified order.

What MATCH is going to do for you is look in a range of cells, either a row or a column that you specify, and it is going to return for you the position of a specific value that you're looking for within that range. You can also have it return the position of the closest value to what you're looking for rather than an exact match.

Note that this is a position that you're getting back. It will tell you that that value you wanted is in the seventh row of the specified range. Or the third column of the specified range.

In and of itself, that's not going to do much for you. But where this becomes incredibly powerful is when you combine the MATCH function with other functions, like the INDEX function, to specify a row number or a column number.

So thinking back to what we did with INDEX, I can go back to that same table I had for student grades and I can use MATCH to look up the row number for each student and then combine that with the INDEX function to pull those student's grades on a specific test.

Here's our data table and result:

	A	B	C	D	E
1			Semester 1		
2		Test 1	Test 2	Test 3	Test 4
3	Student A	82	87	94	92
4	Student B	88	81	84	83
5	Student C	65	68	64	63
6	Student D	98	98	98	99
7	Student E	86	88	84	83
8					
9	Test 3 Results, Semester 1				
10					
11		Semester			
12	Student A	94			
13	Student B	84			
14	Student C	64			
15	Student D	98			
16	Student E	84			

I created a separate table that has each student name in it and then I used the formula

$$=INDEX((\$A\$2:\$E\$7),MATCH(\$A12,\$A\$2:\$A\$7,0),4)$$

to pull the test result from the fourth column of my data range for each and every student without having to know which row each student was in.

Let's break this down.

We start with the INDEX function. We're applying it to the range from Cell A2 through Cell E7. For the row component, which is the second component, I've used a MATCH function. And then for the column component I have the value of 4 which will pull test results on Test 3.

The MATCH portion of our formula is:

$$MATCH(\$A12,\$A\$2:\$A\$7,0)$$

That's saying to look at the value in Cell A12 and to compare that to the values in Cells A2 through A7 and return the row number within that range where there's an exact match to the value in Cell A12.

Pretty cool, huh? It requires a little twisting of your mind to get it to work, but this could be incredibly powerful if you can do that.

A few things to know:

MATCH will look for a numeric value, a text value, or a logical value. It can also work with cell references as we saw above. If you are looking for text and specify an exact match, you can use the wildcards (? or *) to look for approximate or partial matches.

There are three match types you can specify. Using a 0 means an exact match. Using a negative 1 means MATCH will find the smallest value that is greater than or equal to the specified lookup_value. Using a positive 1, so just 1, means MATCH will find the largest value that is less than or equal to the lookup_value.

If you use -1 or 1, you need to sort your data or it won't work properly; it will return a value of #N/A!. For -1, sort your data in descending order. For 1, sort your data in ascending order.

Excel's default is to treat MATCH as if you've specified 1 as your match type, so be very very careful using MATCH since the default match type requires a specific sort order. (I will note here that with all of these lookup functions I far prefer to use them for exact matches, because it's less likely I'll mess something up that way, but there are very good reasons to use them without wanting an exact match. You just have to be more careful.)

Keep in mind, too, that MATCH is not returning a row or column number. It is returning the *relative* row or column number *within your specified range of cells*.

For text, MATCH does not distinguish between upper and lowercase letters.

If there is no match, MATCH will return a result of #N/A!

One of the reasons I included this function was because I saw an interesting use of the INDEX function when paired with the MATCH function recently that used MATCH and INDEX to pull in rank order of 34 different variables for a list of individuals. I'm not going to walk through it here because parsing it out would take about two pages of text, but just suffice it to say that you can get very complex results by using two simple functions like these together.

(If anyone is really curious about what that looked like, you can always email me and I'll send the formula to you. I can't send the worksheet, though, because it's not mine to send.)

THE LEN FUNCTION

Notation: LEN(text)
Excel Definition: Returns the number of characters in a text string.

Those last few were pretty intense, so let's cover a simple one now. The LEN function. The LEN function returns a numeric value representing the number of characters in a text string. (Note that for some languages like Japanese, Chinese, or Korean that you may instead need the LENB function which returns the number of bytes in a text string.)

The count includes spaces as well as actual characters.

You can use LEN with text directly in the function or with a cell reference.

So

=LEN("Alpha")

will return a value of 5 for the a-l-p-h-a in Alpha.

I could also type Alpha in Cell A1 and then use =LEN(A1) to get the same result.

If there is a formula in a cell that is referenced by LEN, it will count the number of characters in the result of the formula.

If a cell is empty or has a "" value, LEN will return a value of zero.

You might be asking yourself when you would use this function. One possibility is when you want to remove standardized text from a longer text string. You could then pair that with a function like LEFT, RIGHT, or MID to extract the remainder of your text.

For example, let's say I have the following entries:

12,500 units
5,122 units
312 units

And I want just the numbers without the space or "units" included.

Assuming that first value is in Cell A1, I could use

=LEFT(A1,LEN(A1)-LEN(" units"))

I could then copy that formula down the next two rows and my results would be:

12,500
5,122
312

This works because all of the entries have the same text at the end, " units". Because the number of units isn't the same between each one, this is probably the only way to trim that off using a function. (You could also use the Text to Columns option on the Data tab as an alternative way to split the number from the units, but it would then require deleting the column of data you don't want to keep so one additional step.)

THE SEARCH FUNCTION

Notation: SEARCH(find_text,within_text,[start_num])
Excel Definition: Returns the number of the character at which a specific character or text string is first found, reading left to right (not case-sensitive).

Another function you could use for tasks similar to the one we talked about above for LEN is SEARCH. SEARCH will tell you the number of the character in a text string at which the text you care about first appears, moving from left to right.

So let's look at that example we used for LEN again. You have three entries:

12,500 units
5,122 units
312 units

And you want to return the numeric values without the " units" portion attached. If you wanted to do that with SEARCH instead of LEN, you could use the following for an entry in Cell A1.

=LEFT(A1,SEARCH(" units",A1)-1)

The SEARCH portion of that is saying to look at Cell A1 and take the number of characters starting on the left that's equal to the place at which the space in " units" occurs. Then you apply the LEFT function to the text in Cell A1 using that value from SEARCH minus 1. (You need that minus one or you end up pulling in the space as well.)

You can also just use the SEARCH function with text entries instead of cell references. So you can have

=SEARCH("mate","teammate")

for example, which returns a value of 5.

If for some reason you didn't want to start at the beginning of your text string, you can use the optional third input to specify where you do want to start.

Let's say I want the location of the first m in the word mamajama that comes after "mama". I could use

$$=SEARCH("m","mamajama",5)$$

and I'll get a result of 7.

Note that that last number in the function, the 5 in this case, is the *start* number. So if I had used 3 as that last input, it would have returned a result of 3 since there is an m in the third position in the word "mamajama".

Also, note that in the above examples that even though we had the search start later in the text string that the number SEARCH returns is still counting from the beginning of the text string.

I could also use

$$=SEARCH("m","mamajama",LEN("mama")+1)$$

if I didn't know how many characters there were in "mama" but knew I wanted to start after it was ended.

Finally, you can use wildcards (* or ?) in the find_text portion of your search. So if you want to find where "cozy" or "cozies" started, you could do so with "coz*", for example, which would capture both options.

If the value you're searching for does not exist in the text string you will get a #VALUE! error. You will also get a #VALUE! error if the start position you give is negative or a larger number than the length of the text you're searching.

SEARCH is not case-sensitive. If you need to do a case-sensitive search you need to use FIND which we'll discuss next.

Also, for languages that use bytes instead of characters you need to use SEARCHB instead of SEARCH.

THE FIND FUNCTION

Notation: FIND(find_text,within_text,[start_num])
Excel Definition: Returns the starting position of one text string within another
text string. FIND is case-sensitive.

FIND is just like SEARCH except it's case-sensitive and doesn't allow the use of wildcards.

Just like SEARCH, FIND requires that you start with the text you want to find and then enter what text string you want to find that text in. It also allows you to set a starting place for your search that is not at the beginning of the text string.

Like SEARCH, FIND also has a counterpart, FINDB, that you can use with languages that look at bytes instead of characters. And like SEARCH, FIND will return a #VALUE! error if the text string is not in the search string or if you specify a start number outside the feasible range.

Let's look at a couple examples that we used for SEARCH:

=LEFT(A1,FIND(" units",A1)-1)

returns the exact same result as using SEARCH did.
So does

=FIND("m","mamajama",LEN("mama")+1)

Where the two are going to differ is in the ability of the SEARCH function to work with wildcards, so

=SEARCH("coz*","teacozy")

will return a value of 4, but

=FIND("coz*","teacozy")

will return a #VALUE! error instead.

They also differ in the ability of FIND to work with upper case versus lowercase letters. So

$$=SEARCH("m","Mamajama")$$

will return a value of 1 but

$$=FIND("m","Mamajama")$$

will return a value of 3, because with SEARCH "M" and "m" are treated the same but with FIND they are not.

Okay? Pretty straight-forward I think.

In and of themselves the SEARCH and FIND functions aren't terribly useful, in my opinion, but they can pair nicely with other functions to do things like trim text, for example.

THE EXACT FUNCTION

Notation: EXACT(text1,text2)
Excel Definition: Checks whether two text strings are exactly the same, and returns TRUE or FALSE. EXACT is case-sensitive.

The EXACT function compares two text strings to see if they're exactly the same or not. This is a function I never really knew existed, but that I've needed before. In the cases where I needed to compare two text strings I was able to write an IF function to do the same thing, but this would've been easier to use.

So I'll walk you through where I've needed this.

As part of my publishing I run advertisements on my books. And there are reports that I can download to see how my ads are doing, but because Amazon is annoying they don't let me run reports for a specified period of time. So if I want to know how my ads did for the last 30 days I need to have a report that I downloaded at the beginning of the period and one that I downloaded at the end of the period. I can then drop those two sets of information into one worksheet and take the difference between them to see how much I've spent and earned on those ads for that period.

But as part of that process I need to be sure that I'm matching up the right entries with one another. When I launch a new ad during a specific month Amazon in all their wisdom will sometimes insert that new ad into the middle of my data instead of at the end. To check if this happened, I usually drop an IF function into my worksheet to make sure all my ads match up. Something like this:

=IF(B2=P2,"","ERROR")

That's saying, do the text values in Cell B2 and Cell P2 match? If so, good. If not, tell me there's an error.

But I could have used this EXACT function instead and written:

=EXACT(B2,P2)

If the two values match it returns a value of TRUE. If they don't it returns a value of FALSE. EXACT is case-sensitive, but will ignore any differences in formatting.

Now, there's one challenge here, which is what to do with the results. They're not easy to visually scan because every cell will have a value of TRUE or FALSE.

And let's say that you have 10,000 entries that you were testing. How can you quickly see if there were any FALSE values in that range?

You could filter the entries. Or you could sort them. You could even use a pivot table to count the number of TRUE and FALSE entries.

You could also use the MINA function to take the minimum value of the range. If all of your values are TRUE, MINA will return a value of 1. If any of them are FALSE, it will return a value of 0.

So if you had this EXACT formula in Column N, you could just use =MINA(N:N) to see if you have any results where the two values were not exactly equal. But that doesn't tell you how many there are that aren't equal. To calculate that you could also use 1 minus AVERAGEA for the range times the number of entries in the range.

So, for example, for a series of entries in Column N you'd have:

$$=(1\text{-}AVERAGEA(N:N))*COUNTA(N:N)$$

where COUNTA pulls the number of entries in the range, AVERAGEA pulls the ratio of the entries in that range that have a value of TRUE, and the 1 minus portion then calculates the ratio of the entries in the range that are FALSE. By multiplying count by ratio we get the actual number of entries that are FALSE.

THE CONVERT FUNCTION

Notation: CONVERT(number,from_unit,to_unit)
Excel Definition: Converts a number from one measurement system to another.

CONVERT is an incredibly useful function that will allow you to easily convert from one measurement to another. (Let me note here that if the conversion you need is just a one-off you can easily use an internet browser to do this. Just type in "20 degree celsius to fahrenheit" in the search bar and hit enter, for example, and the top result or one of the top results will be the answer. But if you have a range of values you need to convert, then this function is the way to do it)

In the help text for the function there is a very long list of options for what you can convert spread across the following categories: weight and mass, distance, time, pressure, force, energy, power, magnetism, temperature, volume (or liquid measure), area, information (bits to bytes), speed, prefix, or binary prefix.

The function itself is very easy to use. The hardest part of using it is knowing what abbreviation to use for your from_unit and to_unit options. You can find all of the available abbreviations in the Help text dialogue box for the function or you can just start entering your function and look at the options provided when you reach that input field.

For example, when you reach the from_unit option you'll see a dropdown menu of the available measurements and you can just scroll down and double-click on the one you need. Same with when you reach the to_unit portion of the function. If you do it this way, the to_unit portion will only display the available options that are in the same category as the from_unit option, saving you the potential of having an error due to type mismatch between your from units and to units.

Let's walk through a few straight-forward examples:

I have a number of friends who live overseas and are always talking about how hot it is there, because it's 40 degrees out. Now, being from Colorado you tell me that it's 40 degrees out I'm bundling up before I head outside. This is because my friends are talking about Celsius temperatures and I'm talking about Fahrenheit temperatures.

So to find what 40 degrees Celsius is in Fahrenheit temperature, you could use:

=CONVERT(40,"C","F")

(That's 104 degrees Fahrenheit and, yes, I'd agree that's pretty darned hot.)

It's as simple as that. The first part of the function is the value you need to convert, the next part is its current units, and the final part is the unit of measurement you need to convert to.

Note that the abbreviation for the measurement has to be in quotes and is case-sensitive.

What about if you know an event is occurring in 1,200 days but aren't sure how many years from now that will be?

You can just use:

$$=CONVERT(1200,"day","yr")$$

Result? 3.285

Those are just two very simple uses for CONVERT. I'll note here that it's listed as an Engineering function and you can see that it might be useful in a context like that if you scroll through the list of available conversion options.

Make sure your units to and from are in the same category or you'll get a #N/A error. Same with if you try to use a measurement abbreviation that doesn't exist. This includes if you input the value using the wrong case. So "day" is a valid unit value, but "Day" is not.

Let me add here, too, that even though it's not on the list of available options you can use "km" for kilometers and "mi" is the miles option you want if you're just trying to convert a good old standard mile to a different distance measurement. (The Help text refers to "mi" as a statute mile.)

Also, in the Help dialogue box they show how to handle squared units by doubling the CONVERT function. So to convert 100 square feet into square meters they say to use:

$$=CONVERT(CONVERT(100,"ft","m"),"ft","m")$$

By nesting the two CONVERT functions that way it appears to work to convert a squared unit to a squared unit.

(I tested it with squared inches to squared feet and it worked on that as well, I'm just using hedging language here because I haven't personally thought through *why* that works the way it does. I'm sure someone more mathematically inclined than I am could write up a little mathematical proof to show me why that works that way, but suffice it to say it does.)

THE ABS FUNCTION

Notation: ABS(number)
Excel Definition: Returns the absolute value of a number, a number without its sign.

Since we were talking math a moment ago, let's continue that with a few mathematical functions that could come in handy at some point in time.

The first of these is the ABS function, which essentially converts any number you have into a positive number. I could see this being useful if you are calculating, say, a ratio of two numbers and it doesn't matter whether one or both of those numbers is negative, you just want the ratio as a positive number.

So, for example, if I had -6 in Cell A1 and 2 in Cell A2 and wanted the ratio of those two numbers as a positive value, I could use:

$$=ABS(A1/A2)$$

And my result would be 3. If I had just divided those two numbers without using ABS the result would have been -3.

That's pretty much it.

(Interestingly enough, if you have numbers stored as text a function like SUM or PRODUCT will not work on them, but ABS still does. So does using the plus sign (+) to add the two numbers or the * sign to multiply them. Odd, but true.)

THE MOD FUNCTION

Notation: MOD(number,divisor)
Excel Definition: Returns the remainder after a number is divided by a divisor.

This next one is a little funky, but could come in handy in certain circumstances. (I suspect its counterpart will be more useful, but I'm covering this one first because there's another way to do the other one that I'll cover after this.)

Anyway.

Sometimes you divide a number and all you really want is the remainder not the integer portion. So it doesn't matter to you that Number A goes into Number B 522 times, you just care about what's left over after that happens.

Well, that's where the MOD function can come in handy. It will take those two numbers and return for you just the remainder.

So, for example, let's say I want to know what day of the week it will be 3,653 days from today and today is January 10, 2019.

I can first divide 3,653 by 7 and find the remainder to see how many days I have left over after however many weeks have passed from today using:

=MOD(3653,7)

What Excel returns for me is the number 6. So now I know that whatever day of the week it's going to be in 3,653 days it's going to be 6 days past today's day of the week.

I can then use the TEXT function (which we covered in *50 Useful Excel Functions*) to take today's date of January 10, 2019 and add six days to it and return a day of the week value using:

=TEXT(("1/10/19"+6),"dddd")

Excel returns a value of Wednesday, which is the day of the week for the date six days past January 10, 2019.

I could combine all of this into one calculation (assuming that the number 3,653 is stored in Cell L2) like this:

$$=\text{TEXT}((\text{"1/10/19"}+\text{MOD}(L2,7)),\text{"dddd"})$$

That's just one example of how you might use MOD. I'm sure if you need it you'll think of it.

The one quirk to the formula is that you don't do your division before you use it. It does the division for you. So your first input is the number that needs to be divided and your second input is what it needs to be divided by. As a result, you will not get the whole number of times A went into B, you will just get the remainder.

Also, you can't divide by zero. And if you're dealing with negative numbers, the sign of the result will always be the same as the sign of the divisor even if both of the numbers you provide are negative.

THE QUOTIENT FUNCTION

Notation: QUOTIENT(numerator,denominator)
Excel Definition: Returns the integer portion of a division.

Now to discuss the flip side of the MOD function, the QUOTIENT function. So where MOD provides the remainder, QUOTIENT provides the whole number portion of the result. Or in math-speak, the integer portion when you divide a numerator by a denominator.

(Don't we feel all smart and fancy now using math terms…)

So if I don't care what the remainder of a number is and just want the number of times X goes into Y, I'd use QUOTIENT.

Taking our example from above, let's say I have 3,653 days and want to know how many weeks that is but don't care if any days are left after that division. I could use:

=QUOTIENT(3653,7)

That returns a value of 521 instead of the 521.8571 I'd get if I divided 3653 by 7.

QUOTIENT does not have the same weird way of handling negative numbers as MOD does. If one of the numbers is negative, you'll get a negative result. If both are negative, you'll get a positive result.

Also, you still can't divide by zero and both inputs need to be numbers but it does seem to work with numbers stored as text.

THE TRUNC FUNCTION

Notation: TRUNC(number,[num_digits])
Excel Definition: Truncates a number to an integer by removing the decimal,
or fractional, part of the number.

The TRUNC function has an end result much like the QUOTIENT function—to just return the integer portion of a number—but it's a function that can work on any number. Meaning it's not limited to a situation where you're dividing two numbers.

Let's walk through this.

$$=TRUNC(3/2)$$

will return a result of 1 just like =QUOTIENT(3,2) will.

Both are returning the integer portion of 3 divided by 2.

But you can also use TRUNC with a cell reference. So if I have 2.34567 in Cell B1, I can write

$$=TRUNC(B1)$$

and it will return a value of 2.

I can also use TRUNC with any calculation within the function. For example:

$$=TRUNC(2.345^5)$$

returns a value of 70 which is the integer portion of the result when you take 2.345 to the fifth power. (We'll cover powers later in this guide, don't worry.)

The default for TRUNC is to round to the nearest integer, but there's an optional input for the function, num_digits, that will let you specify how precise you want your truncation to be. Remember, this is not rounding. This is just chopping the number off at the specified location.

Let's look at some examples.

	A	B	C	D
1	**Test Number**	**Num_Digit**	**Result**	**Comment**
2	**137,254.32451**	0	137254	No decimal places
3		1	137254.3	One decimal place
4		2	137254.32	Two decimal places
5		3	137254.324	Three decimal places
6		4	137254.3245	Four decimal places
7		-1	137250	Truncated without the 1s
8		-2	137200	Truncated without the 10s
9		-3	137000	Truncated without the 100s
10				
11	**132,798.79867**	0	132798	No decimal places
12		1	132798.7	One decimal place
13		2	132798.79	Two decimal places
14		3	132798.798	Three decimal places
15		4	132798.7986	Four decimal places
16		-1	132790	Truncated without the 1s
17		-2	132700	Truncated without the 10s
18		-3	132000	Truncated without the 100s

Here we have two numbers, 137254.32451 and 132798.79867 and I've applied the TRUNC function to each one using different values for the num_digits value.

See how you can cut the number off at any point you want by using varying num_digits values? I can keep the number up to two decimal places (using 2 for num_digit) or I can even have it return a value that's only showing numbers for the hundreds place (using -3 for num_digits).

Also note here that TRUNC does not round numbers. So

=TRUNC(132798.79867,-3)

returns a value of 132000, not a value of 133000 like you would get with

=ROUND(132798.79867,-3)

THE INT FUNCTION

Notation: INT(number)
Excel Definition: Rounds a number down to the nearest integer.

Just like TRUNC, the INT function also returns the nearest integer for a number you specify but it uses a different methodology. It's also not as flexible as TRUNC. It will only return the nearest integer. There is no num_digits option with this function.

The difference between the two is that TRUNC literally just chops off the last portion of a number whereas INT rounds down to the nearest integer. This means that when a number is positive the two functions will give the same result, but when the number is negative they will give different results.

ROUND is another function that returns a similar result to INT and TRUNC, but ROUND will round up or down depending on which number is closest, so sometimes it will return the same result as TRUNC for negative numbers and sometimes it will return the same result as INT. (For positive numbers ROUND will only return the same value as INT and TRUNC about half of the time.)

Let's look at some examples:

	A	B	C
1	**Test Number**	**Function**	**Result**
2	**70.3458**	INT	70
3		TRUNC	70
4		ROUND	70
5	**70.8974**	INT	70
6		TRUNC	70
7		ROUND	71
8	**-70.3458**	INT	-71
9		TRUNC	-70
10		ROUND	-70
11	**-70.8974**	INT	-71
12		TRUNC	-70
13		ROUND	-71

The formulas here for the value in A2 are:

$$=INT(A2)$$

$$=TRUNC(A2)$$

$$=ROUND(A2,0)$$

You can see that when a number is a positive number (the first and second examples), that both INT and TRUNC will return the same value. INT is rounding down and TRUNC is dropping anything after the decimal place, but for positive numbers the outcome is the same. ROUND, however, will round down if the value after the decimal is less than five and up if it's 5 or more. So you can see that for 70.3458 all three functions return the same value, but that for 70.8974 ROUND returns a value of 71 instead of 70.

When the number is a negative number things get even more interesting. INT is always going to round down, which means it will return the next integer away from zero. In our examples that's -71. But TRUNC continues to just chop off all of the numbers after the decimal, so it returns a value of -70 in both cases. ROUND is rounding towards the closest integer so for -70.3458 it returns a value of -70 and for -70.8974 it returns a value of -71.

Which function you use will depend on why you're doing what you're doing. If I was going to be performing ongoing calculations and precision mattered, I'd go with ROUND. But I can see using INT or TRUNC for displaying information. For example, due to the way that books are read in Kindle Unlimited, I sometimes have fractional reads of my titles and I don't want my reports to display 2.645 "sales" of a title. I could easily see using TRUNC or INT to just display 2 rather than rounding up to 3.

One more thing to add here. In the Help text they mention that if you want just the decimal portion of a number and you aren't doing division so can't use MOD that you can combine the INT function with subtraction to do that.

That's not actually true. At least not for negative numbers.

But you can do this with the TRUNC function and it will work for both positive and negative numbers. Simply take the number minus the TRUNC of the number to get the decimal portion. So for a value in Cell A2, you'd use:

$$=ABS(A2-TRUNC(A2))$$

Assuming that the value in Cell A2 is 3.4567 the result you'd get is .4567. Same with a value of -3.4567. I used the ABS function there because otherwise for a negative value in Cell A2 you'd have a negative value returned by the function.

THE POWER FUNCTION

Notation: POWER(number, power)
Excel Definition: Returns the result of a number raised to a power.

I promised we'd cover how to do powers, so let's do that one now.

First, you don't need a function to do powers, you can just use the little carat symbol (^) and input your power that way.

So

$$=3\char94 2$$

returns the value of three squared which is 9.

And

$$=9\char94.5$$

returns the value for the square root of 9 which is 3.

You use whole numbers to take a number to a power and decimals to take the root of a number. You can also use negative powers to indicate that the number is part of the denominator. (So $=3\char94-2$ is the same as 1 divided by three squared or 1/9.)

But the POWER function is there for when you can't hand-write your formula. Say you're working with a table of 10,000 entries and need to perform a calculation that includes taking the values in Column A to a power that you specify. That's when you'd use this.

It's very simple. The first value is the number you want to take to a power, the second number is the power you want to use.

So three squared would be

$$=POWER(3,2)$$

And the square root of 9

$$=POWER(9,.5)$$

I've used squared and square root examples here, but you can use any number you want. So, two to the fourth power is

$$=POWER(2,4)$$

or 16.

The power can also be a negative number which, as mentioned above, will return a decimal value. So

$$=POWER(2,-4)$$

is the same as 1 divided by 2 to the fourth power or 1/16 or .0625.

If the power is 0 then the result is 1.

If you do

$$=POWER(0,0)$$

you will get a #NUM! error. Otherwise it should work with any numbers you give it.

THE SQRT FUNCTION

Notation: SQRT(number)
Excel Definition: Returns the square root of a number.

The SQRT function is a specialized version of the POWER function that only requires one input because it will always take the square root of the number provided.

So

$$=SQRT(9)$$

is equivalent to

$$=POWER(9,.5)$$

If you're writing a long complicated formula and aren't pulling the power to use from your data, it might make sense to use SQRT instead of POWER to simplify things. Otherwise, POWER is the more generic of the two functions and can be used in place of SQRT.

THE PI FUNCTION

Notation: PI()
Excel Definition: Returns the value of Pi, 3.14159265358979, accurate to 15 digits.

The PI function is another function that can make life simpler. If you need to do a calculation that involves the number pi, 3.14 etc. etc., using the PI function will return that value for you accurate up to the 15th digit.

So, for example, the area of a circle can be calculated using pi times the square of the radius. Let's assume radius is in Cell A1.

I could write

$$=PI()*(A1\wedge2)$$

to make that calculation.

Note that when I use the function PI I need to include those opening and closing parens to let Excel know that's what I'm doing. You don't put anything in them, though.

If you just want the value of pi in a cell type

$$=PI()$$

in that cell and hit enter.

THE SQRTPI FUNCTION

Notation: SQRTPI(number)
Excel Definition: Returns the square root of (number * Pi).

I'm sure there's some specific mathematical use for this one, but it's not one I know off the top of my head. What SQRTPI does is returns the square root of the product of a number and pi.

So if you want the square root of pi you can get that with

$$=SQRTPI(1)$$

(You could also get it with $=PI()^.5$)

If you want to use a different number, let's say 3, then you'd write:

$$=SQRTPI(3)$$

That would give you the square root of the value of 3 times pi, or the square root of 9.424778. which is approximately 3.07.

Note that this is not the same value as the square root of 3 multiplied times pi. Nor is it the same value as the square root of pi multiplied times 3.

This function takes the value that you enter, multiplies that times pi, and then takes the square root of the resulting product.

(This is why I'm sure it's part of some common mathematical computation I just can't think of right now. Because why else would you have a function dedicated to something that specific?)

Anyway. If you need it, it's there. But know that you can also just recreate it with something like:

$$=SQRT(X*PI())$$

where X is the number that you want to use.

THE EXP FUNCTION

Notation: EXP(number)
Excel Definition: Returns e raised to the power of a given number.

Since we talked about how to have Excel tell you the value of pi, let's talk about another common mathematical value that you may need, *e*, which is often used in connection with natural logarithms. According to the Wikipedia entry I looked at today, e is an irrational and transcendental number. It has a value approximately equal to 2.718281828.

This value is then used in connection with natural logarithms which are defined as the power to which e would have to be raised to derive a value, x. But don't take my word for it. If you need to use natural logarithms talk to someone who actually uses them.

I'm just here to tell you how to use EXP to derive that value so you don't have to memorize it or input it each time.

If you want the value of *e* for use in an equation, simply use

$$=EXP(1)$$

and Excel will return for you a value of 2.718281828.

You can also, of course, use EXP to get any value of *e* raised to a power, but I wanted to point out that specific use because of the function we're going to look at next, LOG.

THE LOG FUNCTION

Notation: LOG(number,[base])
Excel Definition: Returns the logarithm of a number to the base you specify.

Many years ago when I was still in school we didn't have fancy computer programs that could solve problems for us so we had to learn all about logarithms and how to solve them by hand. I have, thankfully, pushed all those memories into a dark hole. But I still have flashes of base 2 calculations or natural logs. And a vague memory that it had something to do with my math and physics classes.

If you need it, hopefully you have a much better understanding of how and when to use logs than I obviously do, because let me assure you that the Wikipedia entry for logarithms is not friendly to novices or those of us who've forgotten what they learned in high school.

Enough of that digression, let's look at what the LOG function does for you.

The default is to assume that you're working with base 10. So if you don't provide a second value in the function and just write

$$=LOG(10)$$

it will assume that the base you meant it to use is base 10.

That means the answer you'll get is 1.

Because 10 to the what power gives you 10? 1

That's why

$$=LOG(1000)$$

is 3. Because 10 to the what power gives you 1000?

If you want to work with a different base than 10, say 2, you just put that into the function as your second argument.

So

$$=LOG(32,2)$$

69

is asking what power you have to take 2 to to get 32. (That's a mouthful of 2's isn't it?)

Answer, 5.

And if you ever need to use base e and aren't sure how to get the value of e (2.7183), you can always use =EXP(1).

So

$$=LOG(86,EXP(1))$$

will return for you the power to which you have to take e to get a value of 86, which is approximately 4.45.

THE LN FUNCTION

Notation: LN(number)
Excel Definition: Returns the natural logarithm of a number.

If you don't want to use my little workaround with LOG and base e, you can instead just use the LN function. The LN function is essentially the LOG function with a base of e.

So

$$=LOG(86,EXP(1))$$

and

$$=LN(86)$$

will give you the exact same result. If you're going to do a lot of work with natural logs then using LN is probably the better option.

THE LOG10 FUNCTION

Notation: LOG10(number)
Excel Definition: Returns the base-10 logarithm of a number.

LOG10 is the base-10 version of the LOG function, but in this case it's not worth learning in addition to LOG like LN is, because you get the exact same result from

$$=LOG10(100)$$

and

$$=LOG(100)$$

since the default of the LOG function is base 10.
I just mention it here for the sake of thoroughness.

THE FACT FUNCTION

Notation: FACT(number)
Excel Definition: Returns the factorial of a number, equal to1*2*3*…*Number.

Let's continue our exploration of how to use Excel to perform mathematical calculations I learned in school and then promptly forgot but that others might care about, this time with factorials.

Factorials are used when calculating permutations and combinations. Permutations are ordered combinations. So with permutations 123 is different from 321. Combinations view 123 and 321 the same.

Let me give you a scenario. You have three people in a room and you want to know how many ways you could put those three people into order. How many permutations of 123 can you come up with? There's 123, 132, 231, 213, 312, and 321. In total, you have six options.

It's easy enough to calculate manually when you have three people. But what happens when you have fifty people? How many ways can you order those 50 people that are unique?

Fortunately, there's a mathematical shortcut for how to do this called a factorial. Don't ask me how the math works (there's an excellent discussion of permutations and combinations at www.mathisfun.com if you're really interested), but suffice it to say that if you have a group of x values and you want to know how many unique permutations you can make from those x values that you use a factorial.

A factorial starts with x and then multiplies that by x-1 and then by x-2 and so on until it reaches 1. That value is the total number of unique permutations for those x values.

So in our three-person scenario we have 3 times 2 times 1 which is equal to 6 and can be written as 3! where the exclamation mark indicates this is a factorial.

For our fifty-person scenario it would be 50! or 50 times 49 times 48 all the way to 1.

Excel can do this calculation for you using the FACT function. So

$$=FACT(3)$$

will give you a value of 6 which is equal to 3 times 2 times 1.

And

$$=FACT(4)$$

will give you a value of 24 which is equal to 4 times 3 times 2 times 1.

If you try to use a number that is not a whole number with the FACT function Excel will truncate it to a whole number. So

$$=FACT(4.567)$$

returns the same value as

$$=FACT(4)$$

(Note that's a truncation not rounding. 4.567 became a 4 not a 5.)

Also, keep in mind that you can't have a factorial of a negative number and that the factorial of zero is returned as a value of 1 since that's standard practice when working with factorials.

If you want to use a factorial to calculate the number of permutations of a subset of that pool, you can combine two factorials to do so.

So, for example, if my true interest is in how many three-person permutations I can make out of a pool of fifty participants—let's say for assigning 1st, 2nd, and 3rd place prizes—I would take the factorial of 50 (the total number of permutations) and divide that by the factorial of 50 minus 3, or 47. (In mathematical notation that would be 50!/47!)

Doing that would leave me with 50*49*48 which is the total number of unique three-person permutations that I can create from a pool of fifty participants.

This is often written as n!/(n-r)! where n is the pool of things to choose and r is the number of them we want to choose each time. This assumes that there are no possible repetitions—once someone is chosen they can't be chosen again, they are out of the pool.

So you can have #50, #48, and #46 as one choice and #48, #46, and #50 as another but you can't have #50, #50, #50.

So that's using factorials with permutations and without repetition.

You can also use factorials to calculate the number of combinations possible. However, lucky for us, Excel has built-in functions that do all the work for you—COMBIN and COMBINA. Let's talk about those next.

THE COMBIN FUNCTION

Notation: COMBIN(number,number_chosen)
Excel Definition: Returns the number of combinations for a given number of items.

Combinations differ from permutations because with a combination the order doesn't matter. Let's look at our three-person scenario from above. We had the following permutations: 123, 132, 231, 213, 312, and 321, but really all six of those permutations are the same if order doesn't matter. They include 1, 2, and 3 so there's only the one *combination*.

If you were assigning medals, order would matter, you'd use permutations. Did person 1 get the gold, the silver, or the bronze? There are six different ways in which those medals could be assigned.

But if you're building three-person work groups then order doesn't matter and you need combinations. Whether I list Mary, John, or Doug first, I still have a group that consists of Mary, John, and Doug.

So while the permutation of three people is six, the combination of those three people is 1. In fact, if the pool you're choosing from and the group size you want to choose are equal, the combination will always be 1.

Let's say instead that we want to build two-person teams out of those three potential participants. We have the following six possible permutations: 12, 13, 23, 21, 31, 32

But if order doesn't matter then 12 and 21 are the same, 13 and 31 are the same, and 23 and 32 are the same. So in terms of unique combinations, we only have 3.

To do this mathematically, we have to take the number of possible permutations and reduce that number to account for repetition. As we noted above, to calculate the number of permutations for a population of size n and a sample of size r, you can use n!/(n-r)!. To reduce that number so that 123 and 321 are treated the same you then multiply that value by 1/r!.

Which gives you:

$$n!/r!(n-r)!$$

This is also sometimes referred to as n choose r. In our example here, 3 choose 2.

Note that this is how it works when you can only choose each participant once per combination. So this does not have 11 as an option or 22.

Let's see if it works.

Our n! part of the formula is =FACT(3) or 6. That's the total number of permutations for the population.

Our (n-r)! part of the formula is =FACT(3-2) or =FACT(1) which is 1.

Which means our total number of permutations for two-person teams out of a group of three is =FACT(3)/FACT(1) or 6.

We then multiply that by 1/r! or 1/FACT(2). Since 1/(2!) is .5 that gives a final result of 3, which matches what we determined above.

That's the total number of combinations in a pool of three possible choices where we want to choose two at a time and not have repetition.

Good news is you never have to go through that mess again. (Unless it's for a math test.) You can just use the COMBIN function.

You tell COMBIN your population size and then your sample size, like so:

$$=COMBIN(3,2)$$

And it returns your value of 3.

Now, remember, this was a scenario where you can't repeat which one you choose. But if you do want to allow for that sort of repetition then there's a function for that, too, COMBINA.

THE COMBINA FUNCTION

Notation: COMBINA(number,number_chosen)
Excel Definition: Returns the number of combinations with repetitions
for a given number of items.

COMBINA works much like COMBIN but in this scenario you throw everyone back into the pool each time you make a choice. So if you're pulling 2-person permutations from a pool of 3 you not only have 12, 13, 23, 21, 31, 32 you also have 11, 22, and 33 as options.

That gives nine possible permutations. (You calculate the number of permutations with replacement by taking the number of choices in the pool (3) and raising it to the power of the number of items you want to choose (2).)

But for unique combinations there are only six: 12 or 21, 13 or 31, 23 or 32, 11, 22, and 33.

The COMBINA function will calculate this value for you. Simply use

$$=COMBINA(3,2)$$

(You could also reach it using FACT, but that one's pretty complex so I'm not going to walk through it here.)

So. To sum it up.

COMBIN and COMBINA work in situations where the order of your values doesn't matter. In other words, where 12 is the same as 21.

COMBIN is the option to use when you can only choose each value once per grouping.

COMBINA is the option to use when you can choose a value more than once per grouping.

FACT can also be used for combinations but you don't need it for that because of the existence of the COMBIN and COMBINA functions.

What FACT can be used for is calculating permutations. You use permutations when the order of your values *does* matter. In other words where 12 is not the same as 21.

Having said all of this, let me give my disclaimer:

I am not a math teacher. I have not used factorials since high school. If this really matters to you find a better source of instruction than me. The actual use of the Excel functions is very straight-forward.

For COMBIN or COMBINA the first input is the size of the pool you're choosing from. The second input is the number of values you want to choose.

For FACT there is only one input, the number you need the factorial of. What that number will be depends on the calculation you're making and where you're using it.

All other discussion provided here has just been to provide context on why you should care about learning these functions, but do not trust me for your math instruction.

THE PV FUNCTION

Notation: PV(rate,nper,pmt,[fv],[type])
Excel Definition: Returns the present value of an investment: the total amount that
a series of future payments is worth now.

Excel also has a large number of finance-related functions. One calculation that we performed frequently in my MBA program was present value. It's a key component to figuring out how much a company is worth. If this company is expected to earn $100,000 a year for the next five years, what is that worth in today's dollars? Hint: It's not $500,000.

Or another way to use the formula is to calculate what the present value of that loan you're about to take out is. If you're going to pay $2,000 a month at a rate of 8% a year, what is that loan worth today? Would you be better off paying cash if you can?

Luckily, there's an equation for this. And it's available to you through Excel using the PV function.

The function has five possible inputs. Let's walk through each one.

Rate, the first input, is the rate you're paying *for the period*. So if the rate is 8% per year, then that's .08 if all your inputs are annualized. Or it's .0066667 if your inputs are based on monthly payments.

If you were using this to look at valuing a company, then you'd want to use the expected interest rate for the period or the expected return you could get on an alternative investment. Basically, you're asking does it make more sense for me to invest this money at an annual rate of 8% or to invest in this company?

The next input, nper, is the number of periods in your calculation. If we're looking at a 30 year mortgage that you pay once a month, then that's 360 periods. If we're looking at five years of annual payments then that's 5 time periods.

Make sure that for all of your inputs the time periods line up. Don't use an annual rate and then list the number of months and the monthly payment amounts. Or don't list a monthly rate then list the number of years. All of it has to align.

Pmt is actually an optional input. You can choose not to list an amount for pmt and instead list an amount for fv. Pmt is the amount that will be paid for each of the periods just specified. If you do list it, the value you list has to be the same value for each period. This function cannot handle variable payment amounts.

So, in a loan example, you might have 2000 here representing your monthly mortgage payment. For a corporate valuation you might list 100000 here for an annual cash flow from the business of a hundred thousand dollars.

(According to the help text, you'd list any value you're paying out as a negative number and any value you're receiving as a positive number. But I'd recommend doing whatever makes you comfortable and being sure it works with whatever else you're going to do with that number. Just be sure that if you have values for both pmt and fv and that if one is incoming money and one is outgoing money that they have opposite signs.)

Fv is an optional input which represents a value you'll receive or pay out at the very end.

Type, the final input, can be either 0 or 1 and represents when payments are made. If you use 0 or omit this argument then the assumption is the payments are made at the end of each period. If you use 1 then the assumption is that payments are made at the beginning of each period.

So let's put this into practice.

Let's say your buddy owes you $1,000 and he gives you three options.

One, he'll pay you $750 right now.

Two, he'll pay you $100 a month for the next 8 months.

Three, if you can wait three years he'll pay you $1,000 at the end of that period but nothing until then.

(He's not a very good friend. Don't loan him money again.)

Let's assume he'll make good on whatever you choose and that you could invest any funds you have at a rate of 10%.

Which of those payment plans has the highest present value?

The first one has a present value of $750. Cash in hand is cash in hand.

The second one has a present value of $770.81. Not the $800 it sounds like, but more than the $750 you'd get if he paid you today.

We can calculate that using

$$=ABS(PV((0.1/12),8,100))$$

(I used ABS value there because otherwise it returns a negative number and for my purposes that's not what I wanted.)

The third one has a present value of $741.74. You get your $1,000 back but because you could have been investing your money at a rate of 10% per year for those three years it's not worth $1,000 to you today.

That we calculate using:

$$=ABS(PV((0.1/12),36,0,1000))$$

In this one there are not interim payments, just the final lump sum which we put in for the fv variable.

So, between the three options, the best one to choose is option 2, the eight monthly payments of a hundred dollars. But if you play with the assumptions about interest rate or alternative investment, that could change. If you had an opportunity to invest that money today at a rate of 20% then you'd want to choose option 1 because changing the rate from 10% to 20% makes $750 cash in hand worth more to you than $800 paid out over the next eight months.

Note that this is a pretty simple version of a present value calculation since it requires keeping the payment rate and the payment amounts constant for all periods, but it is effective for looking at loans or annuities where that may be the case.

THE NPV FUNCTION

Notation: NPV(rate,value1,[value2],…)
Excel Definition: Returns the net present value of an investment based on a discount rate and a series of future payments (negative values) and income (positive values).

Closely related to the PV function is the NPV function. The PV function takes a standard set of payments and a rate and gives you a present value. The NPV function lets you take a series of payments that can be of different amounts, both positive and negative, and tells you their present value given a specified rate. So NPV gives you more flexibility than PV, but it also requires more inputs because it works with a range of values not just one payment amount or one future lump sum payment.

You could use multiple PV calculations to get the same results as NPV, but using NPV will save you time.

One trick with NPV is that your incoming and outgoing funds have to occur on a regular basis. So, for example, annually. Or monthly. If you have one payment that occurs in January and another in April and another in October, then you're going to want to structure your rate and values to be monthly values with zeros for the months where no payment is made.

Also, any initial inflow or outflow of cash that's made on Day 0 has to be treated separately from the NPV calculation.

So, let's say I have the following scenario:

I am going to pay $15,000 to start a company today. I expect that I will lose $2,500 in my first year of operations and then make $3,500 in the second year, $5,000 in the third year, and $12,500 in the fourth year. Beyond that I'm expecting $0 in earnings.

If I could instead invest that $15,000 at a rate of 8%, should I make the investment?

You can use NPV to figure this out. Put your cash flows in Cells A1 through A4. So -2500, 3500, 5000, 12500. Added up they total to $18,500, more than my investment, but with that 8% that I could earn instead, it might not be enough to justify making the investment.

So I use

$$=NPV(0.08,A1:A4)$$

to calculate what those future cash flows are worth today and I get $13,842.91. I also paid $15,000 to start the business. So net, I'm out $1,157. I could've made more by just investing that money at a rate of 8% for those four years.

But what if that $12,500 came in the first time period? And I didn't lose the $2,500 until year four? So I have 12500, 3500, 5000, and -2500 in Cells A1 through A4? Then

=NPV(0.08,A1:A4)-15000

gives me $1,706 so I'd be more profitable if I started that company than just invested the funds.

You could recreate these results using the PV function, but you'd have to do it with separate calculations for every single payment. (You could also just use payment divided by interest rate raised to the power of the time period for each one and then add all those values to get the same result.) But it's much simpler to just use NPV.

THE FORECAST FUNCTION

Notation: FORECAST(x,known_y's,known_x's)
Excel Definition: Calculates, or predicts, a future value along a linear trend
by using existing values.

An interesting statistical function that Excel provides is the FORECAST function.

Now, one thing to note right up front is that this only works with linear trends. So the plotting example I used in *Intermediate Excel* about calculating time to hit the ground when an object is dropped from different heights would not work with FORECAST since that's not a linear relationship.

Which means you should definitely plot your data before you apply FORECAST to it to see if it's following a general linear trend.

Also, if you have Excel 2016 or later this function still exists but it has technically been replaced with FORECAST.LINEAR since Excel 2016 added the ability to forecast using exponential triple smoothing as well. (Which we are not covering here since I'm working in Excel 2013.)

The way FORECAST works is you give Excel a table of known x and y combinations and Excel then uses those data points to create the best linear fit through the points.

You then tell Excel your x value that you want to predict y for.

Your x value must be a number otherwise you will get a #VALUE! error.

You also must provide an equal number of x's and y's that have values. If they don't match up or one is empty you will get a #N/A! error message.

If there is no variance in your x values you will get a #DIV/0! error message.

If you want to know the formula Excel uses to do this calculation, it's in the help documentation for the function.

Now let's walk through an example. Here's a data table where I've put monthly units sold. Column A is the actual month the sales occurred in, but I can't use that column for the function because the x values need to be a number. So in Column B we have a number that corresponds to each month. Column C has units sold.

	A	B	C
1	**Month**	**Month #**	**Units**
2	Jan-18	1	125
3	Feb-18	2	150
4	Mar-18	3	175
5	Apr-18	4	200
6	May-18	5	225
7	Jun-18	6	250
8	Jul-18	7	275
9	Aug-18	8	300
10			
11	**FORECAST EXAMPLES**		
12	Jan-19	13	425
13	Nov-17	-1	75

You can see the two FORECAST examples below the table.

The first is forecasting into the future. Given the data in the table, what do we predict units sold will be in January, month 13? The answer, 425.

The formula I used here was

=FORECAST(B12,C2:C9,B2:B9)

where B12 is the number 13, for the thirteenth month given our data table values, C2 through C9 contains our y values, and B2 through B9 contains our x values.

Now, one thing to point out here, because it tripped me up the first time I used the function, is that you list all of your y values before you list all of your x values. This was backwards to me since every point coordinate I ever remember seeing was written x, y.

If you look at the data you'll see that I have it structured so that every single month the number of units goes up by precisely 25 units. So if I want to know the number of units in January 2019 given this data I know that it should be 25 times the number of months between August 2018 and January 2019 plus the number of units for August 2018. So 300+(5*25) or 425.

And that's exactly what we get using FORECAST.

The second example I have there is for predicting a value in the past. In this case, November 2017.

This one also required me to make an adjustment I hadn't expected because Excel thinks it's dealing with numbers but I had converted from months to numbers. Meaning Excel was using the value of 0 as a legitimate point and I wasn't thinking that way.

Originally, because November 2017 is two months before January 2018 I used -2 for my x value. But that gave me a wrong answer. I wasn't thinking that December 2017 would have a value of 0 to Excel instead of a value of -1. Once I realized that, I was able to change the value for November 2017 to -1 and it worked just fine.

The function for November 2017 in this example is:

$$=FORECAST(B13,C2:C9,B2:B9)$$

If I'd been using two ranges of numeric values for my x's and y's this wouldn't have been an issue. But it does serve as a good reminder to always, always check your results.

Also, keep in mind that even though my example was custom-built to use exact changes of 25 every period, that FORECAST will work even when the change between periods is not exact. For example, look at the below data and chart of that data:

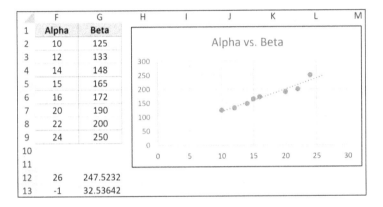

I've added a forecast trendline to the graph to show what Excel is doing mathematically with that data. You'll see that for that last data point, an alpha of 24 and a beta of 250, that the overall trendline actually comes in below the data point.

That means that when we ask Excel to predict a beta given an alpha value of 26 that it predicts a value for beta that is less than the value we have when alpha is 24. With the FORECAST function, Excel is basically moving along that trendline to find each value.

Lastly, I wanted to show you a non-linear scenario like in the example below.

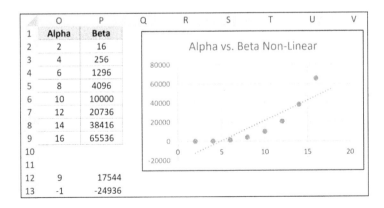

See how the linear trendline misses the actual beta values except for when the alpha is about 6 and 14? If I use FORECAST anywhere except those two points, like I did for 9, the prediction Excel returns will be inaccurate. It's trying to apply a linear relationship to something that is not linear.

This is why you should always, always plot your data first. (I used scatter plots in the two charts above.)

One final note. Even though in the examples above I had the data points sorted by x-value, you don't need to do that. Your data can be out of order and Excel will still be able to work with it effectively.

THE FREQUENCY FUNCTION

Notation: FREQUENCY(data_array,bins_array)
Excel Definition: Calculates how often values occur within a range of values
and then returns a vertical array of numbers having one more element than Bins_array.

In *50 Useful Excel Functions* I covered the functions for calculating average, median, and mode. And as part of doing so I pointed out that one of the drawbacks of even MODE.MULT is that it only cares about the most frequently occurring value or values. So if you have a value that appears 29 times and one that appears 28 times, MODE.MULT will only return the value that appears 29 times.

One way to get around this is by building a frequency table.

Or you can use the FREQUENCY function to pull your x-most-frequent values.

So let's look at that. Here's a data table of values.

	A
1	1
2	3
3	3
4	3
5	3
6	30
7	30
8	30
9	500
10	500

We have the values 1, 3, 30, and 500 with 3 being the most frequent of the values, but 30 coming in close behind that.

If I were to use MODE.MULT on this data range I would get the result of 3 back, but nothing else.

So we want a function that will give us more depth than that. We can use FREQUENCY, but it has its own quirks because it only works if you provide "bins" for it to use. If you don't provide these bins, you'll just get a count of all of your values.

What are bins? Bins are essentially value ranges. In this case I want each of my values in that table to be treated as a separate bin, so I'm going to use Remove Duplicates under the Data tab to copy the entire table and then generate a list of unique values from that table. That will give me my bins.

I can then use the FREQUENCY function to get the frequency of each value in that table.

FREQUENCY is an array function so you have to highlight all of the cells where you want your results to be displayed before you type the function.

In this example, we can highlight Cells D2 through D5 and then type

$$=FREQUENCY(A1:A10,C2:C5)$$

where A1 through A10 is the data and C2 through C5 contain the values for creating the bins. To finish, use Shift+Ctrl+Enter instead of simply using Enter.

This is what we get:

	C	D
1	Bins	Count
2	1	1
3	3	4
4	30	3
5	500	2

I have four 3's, 3 30's, 2 500's, and 1 1 in that data table.

Let's say we didn't use the values to create our bins. Instead I chose to arbitrarily assign ranges at 25, 50, 500, and 1000. Those values are in Cells G2 through G5. I then highlighted five cells and used the following function:

$$=FREQUENCY(A1:A10,G2:G5)$$

This is what we get:

	G	H
1	Bins	Count
2	25	5
3	50	3
4	500	2
5	1000	0
6		0

What's happening here is that Excel is giving a count of all values up to 25, so in this case the five

1s and 3s. Then it's giving a count of all values between 25 and 50, so in this case the three 30s. And then it's giving a count of all values between 50 and 500, in this case the two 500s. After that is a count of all values from 500 to 1000, or 0, and then finally a count of all values over 1000, again 0.

So you can use FREQUENCY for precise counts of each value, like we did in the first example, or for counts across a range of values, like in the second example. You just have to structure your bins correctly.

And remember to highlight enough cells when inputting the function to cover the less than and more than portions of the range. So I had four bin inputs but needed to highlight five cells when I built the second function.

Also, FREQUENCY will ignore blank cells and text, so if you want the FREQUENCY of text values, you can't use it. It only works with numbers.

And remember, this is an array function, so always highlight all of your cells where you want your answers before you input your function and use Shift+Ctrl+Enter when you're done or you won't get the right results.

HOW EXCEL HANDLES DATES

Before we dig into the various date-related functions that Excel has there are a few things it helps to know about dates and how Excel handles them.

By default Excel actually encodes each date as a number starting with the number 1 for the date January 1, 1900 and then moving forward one number at a time for each subsequent date. You can test this by typing the number 1 into a cell and then formatting that cell as a date. As soon as you format that cell as a date you will see January 1, 1900 in that cell. (Unless you're on a Mac, in which case continue reading.)

This is important for a few reasons.

First, it means that Excel does not do well with dates prior to 1900. I learned this the hard way on a work project that had dates back to the 1700s when I found that Excel had converted those 1700s and 1800s dates to 1900s dates after they were imported from a SQL database into Excel. So it's something to keep an eye on if you're working with older dates.

Dealing with future dates is not as much of a problem because Excel can work as far into the future as the year 9999.

Second, because Excel encodes dates as numbers this means that simple addition and subtraction works on dates in Excel. If you want a date fifteen days in the future, you just add 15 to the current date. So say that date is stored in Cell A1, then you'd write =A1+15 and Excel would return a date for you that is 15 days past the date in Cell A1. If you wanted a date that was 14 days prior to that date then you would write =A1-14.

As long as the dates remain in the range of January 1, 1900 to December 31, 9999 you're fine.

There are also functions that specifically exist to do this type of math. For example, the DAYS function which we'll cover in more detail momentarily returns the difference in the number of days between two dates.

Third, the fact that dates are encoded as numbers means that any date functions that mention a serial_number as the input are actually telling you to input the date that you want to use.

Now, to put a wrinkle in this, if you're using a Mac instead of a PC, what I said above about the date range covered by Excel is not accurate. For Macs Excel actually starts with the date January 2, 1904 and moves forward from there. This means that the two systems represent the same date as different numbers. There will be a difference of 1,462 days between how any date is represented by Excel for Windows versus Excel for Mac.

If you're moving files back and forth between the two platforms, Excel is set up to account for this. There's a checkbox for using the 1904 date system and when you open a file created using Excel for Mac that box will be checked already in Excel for Windows so that the dates aren't impacted. If you don't want that, you can uncheck the box under File->Options->Advanced->When Calculating this Workbook.

Another option if you're moving back and forth between the two platforms with the same dataset is to perhaps store your dates as text and then convert them once they're on the new platform. (This may also be a good time to point out that Excel is not necessarily the ideal option for handling large amounts of complex data. It's great for basic usage and calculations but when you really get into data it's probably time to use something else. For example, I've worked with R, Stata, and SQL databases when dealing with large amounts of data.)

This difference between the two systems means that if you try copying data from a file that was created in Excel for Windows to a file that was created in Excel for Mac or vice versa it's quite possible your dates will be off. Same with referencing a Cell in an Excel file that was created on the other platform.

(You can use the Paste Special-Values-Operation option in Excel to paste dates from one to the other. This will allow you to add or subtract 1462 to each date value as you copy and paste it to the other type of file. You can also update your formulas to add or subtract the required number of days if needed. Ridiculous, I know. This is why standardized approaches to data handling are a good idea, but that's what you get when you have competing platforms.)

Bottom line: Be aware of this and check to see if it's an issue when you're working with dates.

Also…

Best practice when dealing with dates in Excel is to enter the four-digit year. So if I want January 1, 2019 it is best to enter that date as 1/1/2019 so that Excel knows exactly what date I want. If you leave off the first two numbers of the year, so use 1/1/19 instead, Excel will convert that to a four-digit year using the following logic:

Numbers 00 through 29 are interpreted as the years 2000 through 2029. Numbers 30 through 99 are interpreted as the years 1930 through 1999.

(I'm not sure what they're going to do about that when we get to 2025 or so and people start expecting to enter 30 and see 2030, but I guess we'll cross that bridge when we come to it. There is a way to change your Microsoft Windows settings so that Excel (and all other Windows programs) uses a different conversion range than that, but the danger is in using files that were created on another computer that was still default range, so I'm not going to cover how to do that here.)

I'd say for now it's something to be aware of, and that you should make sure you enter your dates as four-digit years as much as humanly possible. (Keeping in mind, of course, that dates prior to 1900 won't work as dates in Excel.)

Good times.

Now that we have a basic understanding of how dates are handled by Excel, let's look at some date-related functions.

THE DATE FUNCTION

Notation: DATE(year,month,day)
Excel Definition: Returns the number that represents the date in
Microsoft Excel date-time code.

We're going to start our exploration of the date and time functions in Excel with the DATE function. This is one I don't regularly use but we need to discuss it first because in the help text for most of the date and time functions Excel has a caution that dates used in each function should be created using the DATE function or as results of other formulas or functions. The implication is that if you don't do this your results may not be fully accurate.

In general, I don't think you'll have an issue using a date you've typed in. For example, 1/1/11, 1-1-11, 1/1/2011, 1-1-2011, and January 1, 2011 all work as long as you keep in mind what we discussed above about how Excel handles dates.

But if it's vitally important that your date calculations be accurate then maybe use the DATE function.

So how does it work?

For the most basic usage, you input a value for year, month, and day and Excel turns it into a numeric value representing a date. For example:

=DATE(1900,1,1)

will return a value that displays as 1/1/1900 and is automatically formatted as a date. (At least in Excel 2013. If you get a number back instead, then change the cell formatting to Date.)

There are, however some definite quirks with this function. The worst one is that if you input a year value between 0 and 1899, Excel will add that value to 1900 to calculate your year.

It's the most ridiculous thing I've ever seen, but that's how it works. (An error message would've been better in my opinion.)

So

=DATE(1880,1,1)

which you would hope returns a date of January 1, 1880 will actually return a date of 1/1/3780.

A reminder that if you're going to work with dates in Excel you must drill into your head that they only work between the years of 1900 and 9999. Also, a good reason to always have your dates display with a four-digit year so you can see when this happens, because 1/1/80 looks like it could be 1/1/1880 even though it's actually 1/1/3780.

With the DATE function if you put in a year that's less than 0 or past 9999 you do get an error message, the #NUM! error.

DATE can do more than just create a date from your inputs. It can also take an existing date and by adding values to year, month, and day create a new date. For this reason, you can enter any value you want for month and for day.

If the value for month is greater than 12, Excel will add that number of months to the first month in the year specified. So

=DATE(1900,14,1)

returns a date of 2/1/1901, which is two months into the next year. And

=DATE(1900,38,1)

returns a date of 2/1/1903, which is two months into the year three years from 1900.

If you enter a negative value for month, Excel will subtract "the magnitude of that number of months, plus 1, from the first month in the year specified."

I find that wording horrible. (I promise, I won't be so critical of all of the functions we're going to discuss in this book, but the date functions can be some of the trickiest to deal with in my experience.)

What you have to keep in mind is that when you go backwards, Excel includes the value of zero as a legitimate value. So if I use

=DATE(1905,-2,1)

Excel returns a result of 10/1/1904 which is three months prior to January. To get a date of 12/1/1904, I have to use

=DATE(1905,0,1)

So technically that's not adding 1 to the number of months, it's subtracting 1.
Let's look at

=DATE(1905,0,1)

which gives us December. 0 plus 1 would be 1. That would give us February. What it's actually doing is subtracting an additional 1. So 0 minus 1 gives us -1 months, or December.

The same thing happens with days of the month. If you're going negative you have to adjust by 1 because of the fact that Excel will take a value of 0 as the value for one day prior and then work from there.

I'd be very careful using DATE to go backward for this very reason. It's far too easy to mess up if you're not paying attention, so check, double-check, triple-check your results.

And once again I will urge you to keep it simple and just use DATE, if you choose to use it, to create a date directly by inputting a year between 1900 and 9999, a month between 1 and 12, and a day of the month between 1 and 31.

Now let's walk through the more complex usage for DATE and the reason all the craziness exists.

The DATE function can be used in conjunction with other functions or basic math to create new dates.

So, for example, you can create a date five years from now by taking a date that's in Cell A1 and combining that with the DATE function as well as the YEAR, MONTH, and DAY functions to extract the values for year, month, and date, respectively. This is more precise than adding 365 times 5 days to that date because it won't be impacted by something like leap year.

What does that look like?

Assuming your date is stored in Cell A1 and you want a date five years from that date, you would write:

$$=DATE(YEAR(A1)+5,MONTH(A1),DAY(A1))$$

That's saying, take the year from the date in Cell A1 and add 5 to it. Then take the month from the date in Cell A1 and the day from the date in Cell A1, and build a date with those values.

If Cell A1 was 1/1/2015 you would now have a date of 1/1/2020 which gives us a date exactly five years from January 1, 2015.

If we had instead used five times 365 days and added that to the date in Cell A1, so =A1+1825, we would end up with a date in 2019, specifically December 31, 2019, because of the existence of a leap year in that date range.

So use DATE if you want to create a new date x number of years or months in the future. Use math if you want to create a date x number of days in the future.

Also, just to note that if I had wanted to use the date in the formula for =A1+1825, I would need to use quotation marks to do so, like this:

$$="1/1/2015"+(365*5)$$

Alright, now let's actually walk through the YEAR, MONTH, and DAY functions.

THE YEAR FUNCTION

Notation: YEAR(serial_number)
Excel Definition: Returns the year of a date, an integer in the range 1900-9999.

The YEAR function extracts the four-digit year from a date.

If this matters for you, the dates are treated as Gregorian dates. Even if they're displayed as some other date type, the year that YEAR will return is the Gregorian-equivalent year for that date.

It's very simple to use. You have a date in a cell and then you use YEAR to reference that cell. So

$$=YEAR(A1)$$

will return the year of the date in Cell A1.

If you reference a date stored as text or written in a text format and formatted as text, Excel will still be able to extract the year for you. Assuming, of course, that the date is a valid date to Excel, so has a year value between 1900 and 9999.

If Excel doesn't recognize the date as a valid date, then it will return a #VALUE! error.

You can also enter the date directly into the function, like so:

$$=YEAR("january 1, 2010")$$

$$=YEAR("1/1/2010")$$

$$=YEAR("1-1-2010")$$

Each of the above will return a value of 2010.

Just be sure to use the quotation marks or you'll get a #NUM! error message.

THE MONTH FUNCTION

Notation: MONTH(serial_number)
Excel Definition: Returns the month, a number from 1 (January) to 12 (December).

The MONTH function works much like the YEAR function except it extracts the number of the month from a date instead of the four-digit year. It will also work with a date written as text.
So,

$$=MONTH("December 21, 2010")$$

returns a value of 12.
As does

$$=MONTH("12/12/2010")$$

You can also, of course, use MONTH with a cell reference, so

$$=MONTH(A2)$$

will return the numeric value of the month for the date in Cell A2.
As with the YEAR function, Excel returns a value related to the Gregorian value for the date regardless of the display format for the date.

THE DAY FUNCTION

Notation: DAY(serial_number)
Excel Definition: Returns the day of the month, a number from 1 to 31.

The DAY function works like the MONTH and YEAR functions, except it returns the number of the day of the month for a given date.

So

$$=DAY("June\ 2,\ 2010")$$

will return a value of 2.

And

$$=DAY(A1)$$

will return the day portion of the date in Cell A1.

If the cell you reference has text that can't be recognized as a date you'll see the #VALUE! error message instead.

THE HOUR FUNCTION

Notation: HOUR(serial_number)
Excel Definition: Returns the hour as a number from 0 (12:00 A.M.) to 23 (11:00 P.M.).

Next we have the HOUR function which will return the hour number for any given date/time entry. Now, one thing to keep in mind is that if you enter a date without entering a time to go with it the date is going to default to a time of midnight, or 12:00 AM. If that happens using HOUR will return a value of zero.

Same with the MINUTE and SECOND functions which we'll discuss next.

But if you have entries that include a time of day, HOUR can extract the hour component from that time.

The easiest way to demonstrate this is to combine HOUR with the NOW function. (The NOW function was one we covered in *50 Useful Excel Functions* that returns the time right this minute, down to the second.)

So if it's 1:15 PM and I use

$$=HOUR(NOW())$$

I will get a value of 13.

That's because the hour value that Excel returns is written in military format. Military format assigns a value of 0 to midnight, a value of 1 to 11 for the hours in the morning up until noon, a value of 12 to noon, and a value of 12 + the hour for any time after noon and up to midnight. So 3 in the morning is 3, but 3 in the afternoon is 15. There is no AM or PM used to distinguish morning times from afternoon times.

Now, you already know that Excel assigns a number to each date starting with January 1, 1900. But what we hadn't covered yet is what Excel does with the hours between each day. It turns out that Excel converts those values to decimals. So if there are 24 hours in a day, then each hour is equivalent to .04166667.

The HOUR function can work with that. So

$$=HOUR(.083333)$$

will return a value of 2 since that's the decimal equivalent of two in the morning. HOUR will also work with a time rendered as text.

$$=HOUR("7:30")$$

will return a value of 7.

$$=HOUR("7:30\ PM")$$

will return a value of 19.

THE MINUTE FUNCTION

Notation: MINUTE(serial_number)
Excel Definition: Returns the minute, a number from 0 to 59.

The MINUTE function works like the HOUR function except it returns the minutes for the time instead of the hour.

So

$$=MINUTE("7:30")$$

will return a value of 30.
As will

$$=MINUTE("7:30 PM")$$

This one also works with decimals in the same way that HOUR did. So if each hour is represented by the decimal value of .0416667 then each minute is represented by the decimal value .000694.

That means that if we use the MINUTE function with 15*.000694, which is .010417, we should get a value of 15. And we do.

$$=MINUTE(.010417)$$

does in fact return a value of 15
As does

$$=MINUTE(.510417)$$

Do you understand why?

Because .5 is equal to half of a day and we're only extracting minutes from that number. So .510417 is equal to half a day plus fifteen minutes.

Sorry if that threw you. It was just my weird way of trying to make this one more interesting than it is...

MINUTE also works with cell references. So

$$=MINUTE(A1)$$

will return the number of minutes in the date/time in Cell A1. Which, as mentioned with the HOUR function, will be zero unless you intentionally added a time component to your date.

THE SECOND FUNCTION

Notation: SECOND(serial_number)
Excel Definition: Returns the second, a number from 0 to 59.

To round out this conversation we have the SECOND function that works just like the HOUR and MINUTE functions except it returns the second component of a date/time entry.

For example, I just used

$$=SECOND(NOW())$$

and Excel returned a value of 41 for me because at the time I hit enter we were 41 seconds into that minute. When I just hit F9 to refresh that calculation it returned a value of 15 because we were 15 seconds into the next minute.

You can write a time with seconds as 4:45:30. That last portion represents your seconds component. If you do that, you can then use the SECOND function to extract that.

So

$$=SECOND("4:45:30")$$

will return for you a value of 30.

As with hours and minutes, seconds can also be represented as a decimal. Each second is worth 0.000011574 so

$$=SECOND(0.000011574)$$

will return a value of 1 and

$$=SECOND(0.000683)$$

will return a value of 59.

Also, remember that a date entered as "1/2/2010" or "January 2, 2010" that isn't specifically entered with a time component will have a time assigned to it of midnight and using the SECOND function on a date like that will return a value of zero.

Basically, as with HOUR and MINUTE, the SECOND function will only return a value other than 0 when your date has been specifically set up to include a time component.

THE WEEKDAY FUNCTION

Notation: WEEKDAY(serial_number,[return_type])
Excel Definition: Returns a number from 1 to 7 identifying the day of the week of a date.

The WEEKDAY function is another one that's similar to what we just discussed. But this function identifies the day of the week for a specific date. So does it fall on a Monday? A Wednesday? A Sunday? The WEEKDAY function lets you figure that out.

By default the WEEKDAY function returns a number for the day of the week, so a number between 1 and 7, where 1 is equal to Sunday and 7 is equal to Saturday and each day in between is assigned a number value within that range.

So

$$=WEEKDAY(A1)$$

where A1 has January 1, 2019 in it and that date is a Tuesday, will return a value of 3.
You could also write that as

$$=WEEKDAY("1/1/2019")$$

or

$$=WEEKDAY("January 1, 2019")$$

If you don't like having Sunday be your first day, you can use the return_type input variable to define a different start point for numbering the days of the week.

Using a return_type value of 2 will assign a value of 1 to Monday instead of Sunday and will then number each day of the week from there ending with a value of 7 for Sunday.

So

$$=WEEKDAY("1/1/2019",2)$$

will return a value of 2 instead of the default value of 3.

Using a value of 3 for return_type assigns a value of 0 to Monday on through to a value of 6 for Sunday. So

$$=WEEKDAY("January 1, 2019",3)$$

would return a result of 1 since Monday is 0 which makes Tuesday 1.

Using a return_type value of 12 assigns a value of 1 to Tuesday on through to a value of 7 for Sunday.

And so on. If you look in the help text in the function you'll see that there's an option for every single day of the week to be your starting point using values from 11 through 17 for return_type.

You may be asking yourself, when would I use this function? (Like I did a minute ago.)

One option is to check what day of the week it is and then have different reactions based on that result.

So let's say you run an amusement park and you want to have one set of prices, $24.95, for weekday attendees and another price, $29.95, for weekend attendees.

You could write

$$=IF(WEEKDAY(A1,11)<6,24.95,29.95)$$

That's saying that using a numbering system where Monday is 1 and Sunday is 7 that if the number of the week is 1 through 5 (or Monday through Friday) then assign a cost of $24.95. If it's not, assign a cost of $29.95.

Done. Works.

That's just one way to use it. I'm sure there are more.

THE WEEKNUM FUNCTION

Notation: WEEKNUM(serial_number,[return_type])
Excel Definition: Returns the week number in the year.

The WEEKNUM function is much like the WEEKDAY function except it returns what week of the year a date falls in.

So

=WEEKNUM("January 1, 2019")

will return a value of 1 because that day is in the first week of the year, no matter how you slice or dice it. But, interestingly,

=WEEKNUM("December 31,2019")

returns a value of 53 even though there are only 52 weeks in a year.

This is driven by how Excel defines a week.

The default is for Excel to define a week as starting on a Sunday and only including dates for that year. So in 2019 the first week of that year is considered to be January 1st, a Tuesday, through to January 5th, a Saturday. Week 2 of 2019, if you're using the default return type, starts on January 6th, a Sunday. That means that the final days of the year, December 29th through December 31st, fall in the 53rd week of the year.

Under the default, dates in December will always be assigned to their year even if that means that the WEEKNUM result you get back is 53.

You can use the return_type input option to change how Excel defines a week.

The values of 11 through 17 can be used to start a week on any day from Monday (11) through Sunday (17) but they still keep dates within their year meaning you can still have a week number 53.

The return value of 21 can be used to apply the ISO 8601 standard for week numbering, which starts a week on a Monday and puts the first Thursday of a year in week 1 of that year.

If you use the ISO standard, sometimes the last day of a year will fall in week 1 and the first day of a year may fall in week 53.

For example,

$$=WEEKNUM("12/31/2018",21)$$

will return a value of 1, and

$$=WEEKNUM("12/31/2018",21)$$

will return a value of 53.

THE ISOWEEKNUM FUNCTION

Notation: ISOWEEKNUM(date)
Excel Definition: Returns number of the ISO week number of the year for a given date.

If you need to apply the ISO 8601 week numbering standard, you can use ISOWEEKNUM instead of WEEKNUM with a return value of 21.

So

$$=WEEKNUM(A1,21)$$

is the same as

$$=ISOWEEKNUM(A1)$$

This function was introduced with Excel 2013, so if you're using an earlier version of Excel it's not available. That also means that if you're designing a workbook for use by a group of users and you don't know that they have Excel 2013 or later, then you should not use this function.

THE DAYS FUNCTION

Notation: DAYS(end_date, start_date)
Excel Definition: Returns the number of days between two dates.

The DAYS function allows you to calculate how many days there are between two separate dates. So, for example, let's say it's June 1st and I want to know how many days it is until Christmas.

I can simply write

$$=DAYS("12/25/18","6/1/18")$$

and get my result. (Sorry for you non-U.S. users that think those dates look funny.)

Note here that when I include the dates within the formula itself that I have to use quotation marks around each date.

Another way to do this is to enter each date into its own Cell and then use cell references with the DAYS function.

For example, if I put December 25th into Cell A1 and June 1st into Cell A2, then I could use the formula

$$=DAYS(A1,A2)$$

and I'd get the same result.

Note that with DAYS you're using an end date and a start date. Your end date *can* be the earlier of the two dates if you want. If it is then the result you'll get will be a negative number. So I can have

$$=DAYS("6/1/18","12/25/18")$$

and my result will be -207.

This is one where you can get the same result without using a function. The minus sign will work just as well. So I can write:

$$="12/25/18"-"6/1/18"$$

and it will return a value of 207 just like writing

$$=DAYS("12/25/18","6/1/18")$$

did. I can also write =A1-A2 where A1 and A2 have my dates and it will return the same result as

$$=DAYS(A1,A2).$$

Because Excel stores dates as numbers, you can also just use those numbers in the DAYS function. So

$$=DAYS(5,3)$$

will return a value of 2.

This only works, however, if the numbers provided are in a legitimate range to be a date value, meaning that it will not work with a negative number or one outside Excel's range.

$$=DAYS(-5,3)$$

will result in a #NUM! error.

The DAYS function also works on dates stored as text. For example, if I have "December 25, 2018" in Cell A1 and "June 1, 2018" in Cell A2 and I've formatted both as text, I can still get a valid result from the formula =DAYS(A1,A2). This is because Excel will apply the function DATEVALUE to each entry first.

(As discussed a little later, the DATEVALUE function converts a text entry version of a date into its numeric value. So December 25, 2018 becomes 43459 which is the date 43,458 days after January 1, 1900.)

If you try to use the DAYS function on entries that Excel can't convert into a date, you will get a #VALUE! error. So, for example, if I misspell December in the cell that has "December 25, 2018", the formula can't convert that entry into a numeric value and therefore can't complete the calculation.

THE DAYS360 FUNCTION

Notation: DAYS360(start_date,end_date,[method])
Excel Definition: Returns the number of days between two dates based on a
360-day year (twelve 30-day months).

This next one is a more-specialized function, but it can come in handy in certain situations.

The DAYS function calculates the actual number of days between two dates, meaning that it accounts for the fact that there are 30 days in November but 31 in December and January. However, sometimes you don't want that level of precision. Sometimes uniformity is preferred.

For example, there are certain securities instruments that calculate their payouts using a 30-day month for all months of the year regardless of the actual number of days in that month. This allows interest payments to be the same each and every month.

If you find yourself in a situation like that, then what you'd need to do is calculate the number of days based on the assumption that every single month has 30 days in it. To do this you can use the DAYS360 function.

The DAYS360 function works just like the DAYS function in the sense that it takes the difference between two dates, except it assigns 30 days to every single month not the actual number of days.

Note, too, that it lists the dates in opposite order. So for DAYS360 you list the start date first and the end date second. Also, help text for the DAYS360 function has a caution that you should not use dates entered as text.

You can enter the dates into the formula directly. For example,

=DAYS360("6/1/18","7/1/18")

returns a value of 30.

So does putting 6/1/18 and 7/1/18 into Cells A1 and A2 respectively and then using

=DAYS360(A1,A2)

There is a third optional component to the DAYS360 function that allows you to specify how dates that fall on the 31st of a month are treated. The default method, which will be used if you don't specify a third variable, is what's referred to as the U.S. (NASD) method. Under this method, if the starting date is the last day of a month then it becomes equal to the 30th day of that month.

So, for February 2019, for example, if I put in February 28th and March 15th as my two dates that will return a value of 15 because it's treating February 28th as a fictional February 30th for purposes of the date calculation.

In addition, according to Excel, if the ending day is the last day of a month and the starting date is earlier than the 30th of the month, the ending date will become equal to the 1st of the next month. Otherwise the ending date becomes equal to the 30th of the month.

So

=DAYS360("5/29/19","5/31/19")

returns a value of 2, because it treats May 31st as equivalent to June 1st and then with a 30-day month that means two days between May 29th and the 1st of June.

And

=DAYS360("5/30/19","5/31/19")

returns a value of 0, because Excel treats May 31st as May 30th which means no difference between the two dates.

The other option is to use TRUE as your third variable. This will apply what's referred to as the European method of handling dates that fall on the 31st of a month. If you use this method, any dates that fall on the 31st of a month are treated as if they fall on the 30th of the month.

So

=DAYS360("5/29/19","5/31/19",TRUE)

will return a value of 1 since it treats May 31st as May 30th. And

=DAYS360("5/30/19","5/31/19",TRUE)

will return a value of 0 since, again, this method treats May 31st as May 30th.

(It's a little confusing, but if you need to know this, you'll learn it. And you'll know which method applies to your situation. I hope. My goal here is to just point it out to you so you're aware that the issue exists.)

THE EDATE FUNCTION

Notation: EDATE(start_date,months)
Excel Definition: Returns the serial number of the date that is the indicated
number of months before or after the start date.

The EDATE function takes any given date and gives the date x number of months from that date. It returns the same result as using DATE with YEAR, MONTH, DAY that we looked at above, but it's a lot easier to use.

So, for example, I could use

=DATE(YEAR(B1),MONTH(B1)+6,DAY(B1))

where the date in Cell B1 is June 15, 2018 and I'm telling it to add six to the month value. That will return a date of December 15, 2018, exactly six months past June 15, 2018.

Or I could just use

=EDATE(B1,6)

Now, one thing to keep in mind with EDATE is that it will initially return the serial number for the date, so you need to format that cell as a date or your result will be a number. 43449 in this example.

EDATE also works with negative numbers for the number of months. So =EDATE(B1,-6) will give the date six months before the date in Cell B1; in this example that's December 15, 2017.

Note that EDATE returns the exact same date of the month each time, regardless of how many days are in each of the months in between. If for some reason your date is February 29th and you move in a twelve-month increment it will return the 29th if that's available for that year or the 28th if it isn't.

Also, any month value you use that's not an integer will be truncated not rounded. (So 5.89 would be treated as 5 not 6.)

THE EOMONTH FUNCTION

Notation: EOMONTH(start_date,months)
Excel Definition: Returns the serial number of the last day of the month before or after a specified number of months.

The EOMONTH function is similar to the EDATE function except it provides the last day of the month x months from your specified date. So where EDATE would move from the 15th to the 15th, EOMONTH will move from the 15th to the end of the month, whatever that date happens to be.

Let's look at the example from above where we were working with June 15, 2018 as our start date

=EDATE(B1,6)

returned a date of December 15, 2018.

=EOMONTH(B1,6)

returns a date of December 31, 2018. So the end of that month six months in the future.

=EDATE(B1,-6)

returns a date of December 15, 2017.

=EOMONTH(B1,-6)

returns a date of December 31, 2017. So the end of the month that was six months in the past.

Just like EDATE, the initial value that EOMONTH returns is the number version of the date, so you'll need to format the cell as a date to convert it to a recognizable date format.

And any month value you use that's not an integer will be truncated not rounded. (So 5.89 would be treated as 5 not 6.)

THE NETWORKDAYS FUNCTION

Notation: NETWORKDAYS(start_date,end_date,[holidays])
Excel Definition: Returns the number of whole workdays between two dates.

The final four functions we're going to discuss are all related to one another. NETWORKDAYS has been around for a long time and allows you to calculate the number of whole workdays between two dates, something I needed in my prior career which is how I ran across it the first time.

Basically, it allows you to take a starting date and an ending date and calculate the number of whole workdays between them. But if you're dealing with holidays, too, then you need to tell Excel which days are holidays so it can treat those as non-workdays and exclude them from the count.

Let's walk through an example. (Apologies in advance to non-U.S. folks who'll think those dates look reversed.)

Today is December 21, 2018.

I want to know how many workdays there are between now and when I'm flying to Washington, DC on January 8, 2019.

Let's first just look at the calculation without holidays included:

=NETWORKDAYS("12/21/2018","1/8/2019")

The answer it gives me is 13.

If I look at my calendar I can see that it's including today, the 21st, as well as January 8th. Because there are five days in the next two weeks, that gives us ten days, as well as today, a Friday, and Monday and Tuesday of the week with the 8th in it.

Not exactly between those two dates. It's inclusive of the dates you include in your function. Good to know, right?

Let's test that on a much shorter example:

=NETWORKDAYS("1/7/2019","1/11/2019")

That looks for the number of workdays between January 7th (a Monday) and January 11th (a Friday). The result is 5. So once again, the NETWORKDAYS function calculates the number of workdays "between" two dates and includes those two dates in the calculation.

Now back to the original example:

=NETWORKDAYS("12/21/2018","1/8/2019")

I don't want to include Christmas or New Year's in that count, so I need to include a third argument that excludes them.

The easiest way to do this is to probably have a separate data table where I list all holidays and then I can just use a cell reference to reference the values in that table. In this case, I put the dates in Cells C1 and C2, which then gives me:

=NETWORKDAYS("12/21/2018","1/8/2019",C1:C2)

And the answer it comes back with is 11.

Now, if I don't want today and that last day included, because today is pretty much shot already and that last day I'm traveling and what I'm trying to figure out is how many days I have left to get this book written, I can combine the NETWORKDAYS function with some basic math:

=NETWORKDAYS("12/21/2018","1/8/2019",C1:C2)-2

By adding a minus two to the end of the formula I take out the first and last day from the calculation. Simple as that to account for how the function works. The key is to remember that's how it works so you know if you need to make that kind of adjustment or not.

In the examples above I used a cell range for my holidays, but how do you include more than one date within the function itself? Hint: You can't just use parens like I thought.

You have to use curly brackets around your holiday date entries. Like so:

=NETWORKDAYS("12/21/2018","1/8/2019",{"12/25/2018","1/1/2019"})-2

See the { and the } around the holiday dates of 12/25/2018 and 1/1/2019? You have to use those if you're going to list more than one date for holiday within the function.

Also note that for every date I listed in the formula above that I had to put quotes around it for Excel to recognize it as a valid date.

So that's NETWORKDAYS, but it has one potentially significant limitation. And that's that it treats Saturday and Sunday as weekend days that don't get counted. Well, what do you do if you only want Saturdays excluded? Or if your weekends fall on Sundays and Mondays?

That's where NETWORKDAYS.INTL comes in. So let's talk about that one now.

THE NETWORKDAYS.INTL FUNCTION

Notation: NETWORKDAYS.INTL(start_date,end_date,[weekend],[holidays])
Excel Definition: Returns the number of whole workdays between two dates
with custom weekend parameters.

The NETWORKDAYS.INTL function is a more sophisticated version of NETWORKDAYS that was introduced with Excel 2010. So if you have an earlier version of Excel it's not available to you.

What NETWORKDAYS.INTL does is it allows you to specify what constitutes a weekend. Otherwise it works just like NETWORKDAYS.

So

=NETWORKDAYS("12/21/2018","1/8/2019")

and

=NETWORKDAYS.INTL("12/21/2018","1/8/2019")

will return the exact same result.

But note that the third value you input for NETWORKDAYS.INTL is an optional weekend variable. When you get to this point in inputting your values, you will see a dropdown menu of options you can use to specify what days Excel should consider weekends. Using numbers 11 through 17 allow a single-day weekend and numbers 1 through 7 allow two-day weekends of any consecutive two days in a week.

So let's say that I work in hospitality and that I work weekends because that's when all the customers are in town. I get off Monday and Tuesday of each week. Looking at that list of options, to set Monday-Tuesday as my weekend, I'd need to use a value of 3 for the weekend input variable. It looks like this:

=NETWORKDAYS.INTL("12/21/2018","1/8/2019",3)

Interestingly, the result is still 13, but it's using different dates to get there.

If I expand the function to include my two holidays (which both happen to fall on a Tuesday), I get this:

=NETWORKDAYS.INTL("12/21/2018","1/8/2019",3,{"12/25/2018","1/1/2019"})

and my result is *still 13*.

Remember with NETWORKDAYS it was 11 because the holidays fell on a workday, but because the holidays in this scenario fall on our "weekend" they've already been excluded from our count of workdays and don't need to be excluded again.

Let's walk through another example.

Remember how we used

=NETWORKDAYS("1/7/2019","1/11/2019")

which gave us a value of 5 for the days from Monday through Friday?

Let's write that using NETWORKDAYS.INTL and a weekend that falls on Monday/Tuesday:

=NETWORKDAYS.INTL("1/7/2019","1/11/2019",3)

Since the 7th and 8th are a Monday and Tuesday and therefore get excluded from the count of workdays, our result is 3.

So there you have it. NETWORKDAYS.INTL works just like NETWORKDAYS except it allows more flexibility in terms of determining what a weekend is. The two are not directly interchangeable because of the fact that they put the weekend variable as the third input variable for NETWORKDAYS.INTL which means the holidays are entered in a different order for the two functions. That means you need to know which one you're working with when you build your formula. And if you change from one to the other later, you need to adjust for that.

THE WORKDAY FUNCTION

Notation: WORKDAY(start_date,days,[holidays])
Excel Definition: Returns the serial number of the date before or after
a specified number of workdays.

The WORKDAY function is related to the NETWORKDAYS function. They basically solve for different parts of the same equation. So where NETWORKDAYS calculates the number of workdays between two dates, WORKDAY calculates what date it will be in x workdays.

So you have x-y=z and one function is solving for y and the others is solving for z. But be careful with that. Because they actually treat the dates differently, as you'll see in a second, so they don't actually fit together that neatly.

NETWORKDAYS includes the start date in its count, but WORKDAY does not.

Let's walk through an example.

Say we're on a project and I ask someone how long it will take for them to complete their portion of the project and they tell me ten days. It's currently December 21st. When can I expect that person to be done with their portion of the project, knowing that they are not going to work weekends or holidays?

I can use:

=WORKDAY("12/21/2018",10,{"December 25, 2018","January 1, 2019"})

So, starting today, moving ten workdays into the future, and excluding Christmas and New Year's, what day is that going to be?

According to the function, it will be January 8, 2019.

Let's see if that makes sense:

Between now and then we have December 21st, December 24th, December 26th through December 28th, December 31st, January 2nd through January 4th, and January 7th and 8th as workdays that are not holidays.

That's actually 11 days. But remember what I said before? Excel doesn't count your start date. That's unlike how NETWORKDAYS works, right?

Let's test that some more.

If we use

$$=WORKDAY("1/7/2019",5)$$

what do we get?

A date of 1/14/2019, which is the next Monday. Same issue. We end up going across six workdays.

How about

$$=WORKDAY("1/7/2019",1)$$

So just one day?

That gives us 1/8/2019, which makes it pretty clear that WORKDAY is adding that number of days onto the current date without including the current date in its count of available days.

So going back to our original example, what if it's first thing in the morning and you know that person will be working on that project today, so you want to adjust for that?

Then you'd basically have to do either:

$$=WORKDAY("12/21/2018",10,\{"December\ 25,\ 2018","January\ 1,\ 2019"\})-1$$

Or you'd have to use 10-1 days in your function, like so:

$$=WORKDAY("12/21/2018",9,\{"December\ 25,\ 2018","January\ 1,\ 2019"\})$$

Of course, there's nothing wrong with having a little wiggle room in a project timeline, so I might just leave it as is, but it's good to know that's how this function works in comparison to the NETWORKDAYS function. Because if for some reason you're using both of them on the same project and not adjusting for the difference, you may have these one-day discrepancies that can cause an unnecessary misunderstanding.

Alright. Just like NETWORKDAYS has a new and improved version that allows more flexibility, so does WORKDAY. Let's cover that one next.

THE WORKDAY.INTL FUNCTION

Notation: WORKDAY.INTL(start_date,days,[weekend],[holidays])
Excel Definition: Returns the serial number of the date before or after a specified number of workdays with custom weekend parameters.

WORKDAY.INTL works just like WORKDAY, except it allows for customized weekend parameters. So

=WORKDAY.INTL("12/21/2018",10,1,{"December 25, 2018","January 1, 2019"})

gives the same result as

=WORKDAY("12/21/2018",10,{"December 25, 2018","January 1, 2019"})

And just like with NETWORKDAYS.INTL, when you get to that third input variable you will see a list of available options for your weekend. Values of 1 through 7 let you set a two-day weekend using any two continuous days of the week. 11 through 17 let you set a single-day weekend.

You can also create a completely customized set of weekend days if you want using a binary string of numbers to represent workdays or weekend days where 1 is a non-workday and 0 is a workday and you start the string with Monday.

So in the below example I have Monday, Tuesday, Wednesday, Thursday as workdays, then an off day on Friday, then a workday on Saturday, then a non-workday on Sunday.

=WORKDAY.INTL("1/7/2019",1,"0000101")

That returns a value of January 10, 2019 because I have the Monday through Wednesday (the 7th, 8th, and 9th) designated as non-workdays.

Also, because weekend is the third variable and then holidays is the fourth for WORKDAY.INTL, you need to know if you're working with WORKDAY or WORKDAY.INTL when you build the function since holidays are in a different location in the two functions.

Finally, WORKDAY.INTL wasn't introduced until Excel 2010, so if you have an earlier version of Excel it won't be available to you. If you have a more recent version of Excel it probably makes the most sense to use WORKDAY.INTL all the time even when you don't need a customized weekend parameter. If you do that, just make sure to enter 1 as your weekend parameter to get a standard Saturday/Sunday weekend when you include holidays.

OTHER FUNCTIONS

That's it for this guide to functions. There are many, many more functions in Excel, including the fifty I already covered in *50 Useful Excel Functions*.

And chances are there's at least one I didn't cover in either book that you'll need at some point.

Hopefully, though, you now have enough understanding of Excel functions to feel comfortable with how they work and to be able to work with one that's new to you.

I also hope this has further demonstrated the potential power and breadth of Excel. Don't be afraid to explore the program and see if it has what you need, because chances are it does.

Next I'm going to talk briefly about how to combine functions within a formula as well as the various error messages and what they mean. I'll also cover what to do when your formula isn't working.

If you already read *50 Useful Excel Functions*, no need to read these sections again. It's the same material.

COMBINING FUNCTIONS

The functions we discussed in this guide are powerful in their own right, but where the real power of Excel can come into play is when you combine functions.

As I mentioned with INDEX and MATCH, each one seems somewhat limited by themselves, but I saw them combined to create a very powerful data table listing rank order for thirty-four different attributes for a group of individuals.

And if you look back at the examples we used in the DATE function, you can see how useful it can be to combine, in that case, four functions in one formula.

So if you find yourself using multiple columns to perform multiple steps maybe see if you can instead combine those steps into one.

The key to keep in mind when combining functions is that only the beginning of the formula requires an equals sign. After that first function or value you just list the function name followed by an opening paren when you need to use a different function within your formula.

And also, to be careful of your paren and comma placement when using multiple functions within a formula.

(And if you're doing calculations and facing a significant file size issue and are using Excel 2013 or later, you might want to explore array formulas a bit more. This is not my area of expertise, but from the little I read about them it appears they can save a lot of file space for repetitive calculations.)

WHEN THINGS GO WRONG

Chances are if you work with formulas enough that you will run into some error messages.

You might see a #DIV/0! or a #REF! or a #VALUE! or a #N/A or a #NUM! error. It happens. Sometimes you'll realize exactly what you did, but at other times it's going to be a puzzle.

So let's me see if I can help a bit.

#REF!

If you see #REF! in a cell it's probably because you just deleted a value that that cell was referencing. So if you had =A1+B1+C1+D1 in a cell (and I do have something similar to this in my budget worksheet), and then you deleted Column C that would create a #REF! error. Excel won't adjust the formula and drop the missing value, it will return this error message instead.

To see where the cell generating the error was in your formula, double-click in the cell with the #REF! message. This will show you the formula, including a #REF! where the missing cell used to be.

So you'll see something like =A1+B1+#REF!+D1 and you'll know that the cell you deleted was used as the third entry in that formula. If it's something like the example I just gave you where you just need to delete that cell reference, do so. Turn it into =A1+B1+D1. But you may also realize that your formula now needs to reference a different cell. If so, replace the #REF! with that cell reference. Hit enter when you've made your changes and you're done.

(This is also a good time for using Ctrl +Z if you thought you were deleting a blank cell and didn't realize it was being used in a formula and are okay with bringing that cell back.)

#VALUE!

According to Excel, a #VALUE! error means you typed your formula wrong or you're referencing a cell that's the wrong type of cell.

If you're using dates, see if the date is left-aligned. If it is, then chances are Excel is treating the date as a text entry not a date entry. That means subtraction won't work on it.

Same with numbers. If you use SUM and get this error on a range of numbers make sure that they're formatted as numbers and not text. (This shouldn't be a common problem, but could be if you've imported a data file from elsewhere.)

It can also mean that you have non-standard regional settings and that your minus sign is being used as a list separator (rather than the more standard, at least in the U.S., comma).

Or it can mean that you're referencing a data source that is no longer available like another workbook that was moved.

#DIV/0!

This is a common error to see if you've written a formula that requires division. If I input the formula =A1/B1 and there are no values in Cells A1 and B1, Excel will return #DIV/0!

You need a numeric value for your denominator to stop this from happening. (The numerator can be blank, but not the denominator.)

I usually use IF functions to suppress the #DIV/0! when I have a data table where values haven't been inputted yet. So I'll write something like =IF(B1>0,A1/B1,"").

Just be sure if you do that that the IF condition makes sense for your data. (In the example I just gave, any negative number would also result in a blank cell.)

#N/A

According to Excel, a #N/A error means that Excel isn't finding what it was asked to look for. In other words, there's no solution. This occurs most often with the VLOOKUP, HLOOKUP, LOOKUP, and MATCH functions. You tell it to look for a value in your table and that value isn't in your table.

This can be valuable information that perhaps points to a weakness in your data or your function. For example, it could indicate that the data in your lookup table is in a different format from the data in your analysis table. Or that there are extra spaces in the entries in one or the other table

But if you know this is going to happen and don't want to see the #N/A in your results, you can use the IFERROR function to suppress that result and replace it with a zero, a blank space, or even text. Just be careful, because IFERROR will replace all error messages and that may not be what you want.

#NUM!

According to Excel, you will see this error when there are numeric values in a formula or function that aren't valid. The example Excel gives involves using $1,000 in a formula instead of 1000, but when I just tried this to validate it Excel wouldn't even allow me to use that formula, it wanted to fix the formula for me as soon as I hit Enter. So this may be more of an issue in older versions of Excel.

Excel will also return this error message if an iterative function can't find a result or if the result that would be returned by the formula is too large or too small. (If you're running into this error for those reasons chances are you're doing some pretty advanced things, so we're not going to worry about that here.)

Circular References

Excel will also flag for you any time that you write a formula that references itself. (I do this on occasion without meaning to.) For example, if in Cell A5 you type =SUM(A1:A5), when you hit

Enter Excel will display a dialogue box that says "Careful, we found one or more circular references in your workbook that might cause your formulas to calculate incorrectly."

Say OK and then go back to the cell with the formula and fix the issue.

Keep in mind that sometimes a circular reference error can be generated by an indirect circular reference, so you're referencing a cell that's referencing another cell and it's that other cell that's the issue.

If you can't figure out the cause and Excel doesn't "helpfully" start drawing connections on your worksheet to show it to you, in newer versions of Excel you can go to the Formulas tab and under Formula Auditing click on Trace Precedents to see what values are feeding that cell.

(Usually when this happens I know exactly what I did and it's just a matter of getting Excel to stop trying to fix it for me so I can make the correction myself. YMMV.)

Too Few Arguments

I also on occasion will try to use a function and get a warning message that I've used too few arguments for the function. When that happens check that you've included enough inputs for the function to work. Anything listed that isn't in brackets is required. So =RANDBETWEEN(bottom, top) requires that you enter values for both bottom and top but =CONCATENATE(text1, [text2],…) only requires one input.

If that's not the issue make sure that you have each of the inputs separated by commas and that your quotation marks, if there are any, are in the right places.

General Wonkiness

Sometimes everything seems fine but the formula just doesn't seem to be giving the right answer. If it's a complex formula, break it down into its components and make sure that each component works on a standalone basis.

You can also double-click on the cell for a formula and Excel will color code each of the separate components that are feeding the formula and also highlight those cells in your worksheet. Confirm that the highlighted cells are the ones you want.

For formulas you copied, verify that none of your cell ranges or cell references needed to be locked down but weren't. (I do this one often.) If you don't use $ to lock your cell references, they will adjust according to where you copied that formula. If that's what you wanted, great. If it isn't, fix it by going back to the first cell and using the $ signs to lock the cell references or by changing the cell references in the location you copied the formula to so that it works.

And, as we've seen here, sometimes there are choices you can make with a function that impact the outcome. So the value RANK will return depends on whether you tell Excel to look at your data in ascending or descending order. If you're working with a function you're not familiar with, open the Excel Help for the function and read through it. If that doesn't help, go to the website. If that doesn't help, do an Internet search to see if someone else has had the same issue.

CONCLUSION

So that's it for this guide. There are many more functions that I did not cover here. Excel is incredibly broad in what it can do, but also incredibly specialized at times.

If you can think of it, chances are there's a way to do it in Excel. So don't be afraid to go to Insert Function and poke around to see what's possible.

(And if there isn't a function for what you want, you can always learn how to write your own macros in Excel. Although be careful with those. And don't look to me for that one.)

There are some more advanced aspects to working with formulas and functions in Excel that I didn't cover here or brushed past. Things like named ranges and array formulas. If you want to learn about those, start with the Excel Help function and go from there.

I find that I take things past the basic level when I need to do something specific, so I go looking for that solution that I need. If you want to be more systematic about it, there are definitely exhaustive guides out there that will cover everything for you.

And if you have a specific issue or question, feel free to reach out to me. mlhumphreywriter@gmail.com. I'm happy to help. I don't check that daily, but I do check it often and will reply.

I hope this was helpful for you. Good luck with it! Remember, save your raw data in one place, work on it in another, take your time, check the individual components of complex formulas, check your threshold cases, and Ctrl + Z (Undo) is your friend.

APPENDIX A: CELL NOTATION

If you're going to work with functions in Excel, then you need to understand how Excel references cells.

Cells are referenced based upon their column and their row. So Cell A1 is the cell in Column A and Row 1. Cell B10 is the cell in Column B and Row 10. Cell BC25232 is the cell in Column BC and in Row 25232.

If you want to reference more than one cell or cell range in a function then you can do so in a couple of ways. To reference separate and discrete cells, you list each one and you separate them with a comma. So (A1, A2, A3) refers to Cells A1, A2, and A3.

When cells are touching you can instead reference them as a single range using the colon. So (A1:A3) also refers to Cells A1, A2, and A3. Think of the colon as a "through".

You don't have to limit this to a single row or column either. You can reference A1:B25. That refers to all of the cells between Cell A1 and Cell B25. That would be all cells in Column A from Cell A1 through Cell A25 as well as all cells in Column B from Cell B1 through Cell B25.

When you note a range the left-hand cell that you list (A1) is the top left-most cell of the range and the right-hand cell you list (B25) is the bottom right-most cell of the range.

You can also reference an entire column by just using the letter and leaving off any numbers. So C:C refers to all cells in Column C.

And you can do the same for a row by leaving off the letter. So 10:10 refers to all the cells in Row 10.

If you ever reference a cell in another worksheet or another workbook, this also needs to be addressed through cell notation.

For a cell in another worksheet, you put the sheet name as it appears on the worksheet tab followed by an exclamation point before the cell reference. So Sheet1!B1 is Cell B1 in the worksheet labeled Sheet 1.

For another workbook you put the name of the workbook in brackets before the worksheet name. So [Book1]Sheet2!$D$2 refers to Cell D2 in the worksheet labeled Sheet 2 in the workbook titled Book 1.

(I should note here that I think it's a bad idea to reference data in another workbook due to the odds that the formula/function will break as soon as that other workbook is renamed or moved to a new location and that I generally don't think it's worth doing.)

Now, before you start to panic and think you need to remember all of this and that you never will, take a deep breath. Because when you're writing a formula you can simply click on the cells you need when you need them and Excel will write the cell notation for you.

It's just useful to know how this works in case something doesn't work right. (And even then you can still use Excel to show you what each cell reference is referring to. Just double-click on the formula and Excel will color code the cell references in the formula and put a matching colored border around the cells in your worksheet.)

ALPHABETICAL LISTING OF FUNCTIONS COVERED

ABOUT THE AUTHOR

M.L. Humphrey is a former stockbroker with a degree in Economics from Stanford and an MBA from Wharton who has spent close to twenty years as a regulator and consultant in the financial services industry.

You can reach M.L. at mlhumphreywriter@gmail.com or at mlhumphrey.com.

www.ingramcontent.com/pod-product-compliance
Lightning Source LLC
LaVergne TN
LVHW082035050326
832904LV00005B/180